ASPARAGUS, ALL WAYS

...always

Cookbook Committee

Glenda Hushaw

Barbara Hafley

Jan Moore

Maureen Mullen

Trish Ratto

Joyce Speckman

Yvonne Calderone

Illustrations by Bill Kobus

CELESTIAL ARTS
P.O. Box 7327
Berkeley, California 94707

Cover art and interior illustrations by Bill Kobus
Cover design by Ken Scott

Library of Congress Cataloging-in-Publication Data

The Asparagus cookbook.

Includes index.
1. Cookery (Asparagus)   I. Stockton Asparagus Festival (Calif.)
TX803.A8A86   1987   641.6'531   86-26918
ISBN 0-89087-487-5 paperback
ISBN 0-89087-537-5 spiral bound

Manufactured in the United States of America
2   3   4   5   91   90   89   88

FESTIVAL

DEDICATION

This cookbook is dedicated to the 1st Annual Stockton Asparagus Festival, a community-wide celebration of both spring and the asparagus harvest.

Community projects, through the work of charitable groups and service organizations will benefit from the proceeds derived from the festival. This festival owes its success to a very strong and supportive volunteer group coupled with the cooperation of many suppliers and service companies.

The Stockton Asparagus Festival is centered around deliciously prepared foods and delightful entertainment for the entire family.

The idea for this festival was conceived by Joe Travale, Executive Director, Stockton-San Joaquin Convention and Visitors Bureau.

CONTENTS

This collection of recipes was gathered from the files of the California Asparagus Growers' Association, families of the 1985 Board of Directors, friends and relatives.

We wish to express our appreciation to all those individuals who contributed their time, energy, and ideas toward the completion of this cookbook. A very special thanks is expressed to all those who shared their personal recipes.

Treat yourself to the "Cadillac" of vegetables—and enjoy!

                            —the Cookbook Committee

Asparagus, the King's Ransom

A Brief History

From the edge of civilization poets have sung the song of asparagus. Artists have painted it; craftsmen have recreated it; photographers have captured it; healers have prescribed it; and epicures have sighed over it. Even kings have been inspired by asparagus, one of nature's most beautifully designed vegetables. Evocative, lean, richly colored and so pleasantly textured, asparagus has a mythology all its own.

Because asparagus has been found growing wild in so many places about the world, there are many opinions as to its actual place of origin. There are scholars who would place this tasty member of the lily family in the eastern Mediterranean area or in Asia Minor. Others say East Central Europe is the ancestral home of asparagus. We do know, however, that it has been cultivated for at least 2,500 years.

The Greeks and Romans enjoyed asparagus as a food and valued it for supposed medicinal properties as well. Early records suggest its value in preventing bee stings, aiding heart ailments, dropsy and toothaches. Teas and syrups were made from all parts of the plant. If you were sick, you might drink it, bathe in it, inhale it, use it as a mouthwash, or in a skin plaster. Asparagus was also prized. . .as an aphrodisiac.

We know that asparagus is a good source of vitamins A and C and of the minerals potassium and phosphorous. Modern medicine uses the root of the plant as a diuretic. Beautiful and delicious, asparagus is also low in calories. . .when left alone.

By the time of the Renaissance the growing beds of Northern Italy were famous. More than one historian has written of the asparagus of Ravenna where three stalks easily made a pound. And Louis XIV of France gave land and a title to his gardener who found a way to provide the monarch asparagus year-around. He did so by building "Stove Houses" and heating the beds inside. It wasn't long after this that the Germans began producing white asparagus—still considered a delicacy in many parts of the world.

The first hardy souls to pioneer America had the good taste to bring asparagus with them. Some say the English brought it over, others say it was the Dutch. It probably doesn't matter. The cultivation of asparagus in New England was recorded in the 1870s.

With the movement west came hardy and industrious individuals—people who were farmers, entrepreneurs, speculators. In the California heartland they found soils of extraordinary variety and composition. And the climate was as challenging. To understand and appreciate this land's potential for productivity took a wonderful act of imagination on the part of agricultural interests. Here, at the confluence of California's two greatest rivers, the Sacramento and the San Joaquin, they found the rich peat of the delta lands. Here was an agrarian frontier to conquer.

As is typical of developing countries, wheat was the first major crop to be farmed by the Americans in Central California. There was a market for it; there was money to be made. As farmers began to understand the nature of the soil and learned how to bring water to their land, and as the railroads became more accessible, other crops were planted. Fruit and grapes were soon successfully grown.

All the while experimentation was being accomplished by men of incredible skill and experience. The land soon brought a cosmopolitan population which planted orchards and a great variety of vegetables in what has proven to be amongst the richest soils in the world.

The lands of the delta were reclaimed in the 1850s. Mighty dredging machines built levees to hold back seasonal floods from tracts of fertile land destined to cultivation. By 1875 some 89 distinct crops could be found growing on these man-made tracts and on natural delta islands.

The earliest recorded growing of asparagus in California was in the northern delta in 1852. The market was strictly local until August, 1900. On that date the first trainload of asparagus was sent east. Shipped from the Hickmott Cannery on Bouldin Island, the twenty carloads began a marketing revolution. When he started his business in 1892, Robert Hickmott had only the crudest of equipment and a fierce determination. He learned by trial and error in a cannery setup under the willow trees. With the easy and regular availability of canned asparagus Americans across the country fell under the spell of nature's most perfect vegetable.

In 1919, Thomas Foon Chew built the Bayside Cannery at Isleton. Foon brought to the delta years of experience in the cannery business. His father founded the Bayside Cannery in Santa Clara County in the late 19th Century. In the delta, from acquired acreage to guarantee his supply and with the genius of William de Back, Foon devised and built asparagus sorting and processing equipment which was, in effect, the prototype of that found in today's canneries. Because the peat soil was soft and retained its moisture, ideal for the formation and nurturing of tender stalks, Foon's Bayside Can-

2

nery became the first cannery to package green asparagus. It wasn't long before Tom Foon had earned the title of Asparagus King. At the peak of operation, Bayside's canning volume was over six hundred thousand cases a year.

Bayside Cannery was wisely located on a ten-acre site in what soon became the asparagus center of the world. With the canning facility Foon built warehouses, cabins, homes, apartment-style quarters, bunk houses and boarding rooms to accommodate about 500 workers. Many of the workers would rise before 6 a.m., harvest asparagus, then return to the cannery to help process the product. The work was hard but the wages were fair and the Chinese were pleased to have the opportunity to earn a living. During harvest Foon gave his workers only spending money. This kept them on the job until the work was done. They then received the balance of their pay. By the time winter came many of the workers were broke. Foon loaned them money knowing that the debt would bring them back to work when the season began again.

Scows, barges and riverboats brought asparagus from the field to the cannery. Later, Model A Fords traveled newly graded dirt roads across the delta. Processed asparagus was shipped by rail to the mid-west and by boat to the bay area. Steamships carried the product to eastern markets. The Delta King and Delta Queen, magnificent stern-wheeled riverboats launched in Stockton in 1925, hauled the bulk of the canned products daily to Sacramento and then on to the bay area for transhipment.

Promoters of the industry grossly exaggerated the amount of land dedicated to growing asparagus. The effect was to bring huge amounts of foreign money into the delta. Additional lands were reclaimed and land owners turned much of their property over to tenants. This brought additional Chinese, Hindu, Japanese, Italian and Irish into the area.

In 1903 nearly 6,000 acres were planted to asparagus in the San Joaquin-Sacramento delta region. In 1984 over 23,259 acres representing a San Joaquin County market value of $28,017,000 were under cultivation. California produces over 70 percent of the nation's fresh market asparagus. Of that production, most is cut in the delta.

For better than a century the ingenuity of the California farmer, assisted by state and university scientists, has improved the quality of the vegetable and the productivity of the land. Growers and gourmands are the new poets singing of the development of hybrids with greater yield and large, tight-tipped spears.

The method by which asparagus is planted, grown and harvested is much the same today as it was a hundred years ago. Horses wearing specially designed peat shoes have been replaced by the track-laying caterpillar tractor of Stockton's Benjamin Holt and later, by other sophisticated vehicles. Hybrid plants with greater yield and disease resistance have replaced the early plants. The balance of production is a slice of history preserved in practice.

Asparagus seeds are planted in a bed where they produce crowns with many roots. After about twelve months these crowns are separated and transported in a burlap sack by a laborer to a "mother field" where each is set into a carefully prepared furrow, bud side up, for the productive span of the plant's life. About 4 inches of dirt cover the plant. After 9 or 10 months of growth, the crown has produced a fern which reaches about 3 feet in height.

The asparagus fern brings nutrients to the crown which initially produces up to 16 buds. After the first frost the fern dies. The farmer then shreds and discs the fern to bring additional nutrients to the soil. The following spring the bed is harvested 6 or 7 times. Each year the crown enlarges. By the third year the cutting cycle lasts between 60 and 65 days. In the fourth year the cutting cycle lasts 90 days.

There's a saying in the delta, "if you can get 90 degrees, you can cut every day." Farmers easily remember cutting on the evening of a 90-95 degree day...after a morning cut. "Why I've seen asparagus grow 7 inches in a day," recalls one grower. Filipino laborers used to wear flashlights attached to their hats like miners. They'd move through the field before daylight to avoid the often intense heat of the Delta.

Asparagus is cut approximately two inches below the soil with a knife that is about 36 inches long. Fresh market spears are cut 10 to 12 inches long. The diameter of the spear depends upon the success of the grower in keeping the proper amount of soil on top of the crown. This provides resistance to the spear, forcing it to push through the soil widening its stalk in the process.

Freshly cut asparagus is picked up by a crewman on a sled, tiered facing one direction, separated by burlap to protect the tip, and then removed to a washer on a conveyor belt. In the early days horses would take the sleds from the field to the shed and return with an empty sled...without a teamster. After washing, the asparagus is graded by size: colossal, jumbo, large, standard, small; and then packed into bundles which are tied with twine. All by hand. Now the asparagus is ready for market.

Each year for up to 10 years the cycle is repeated. Chinese laborers have been replaced by Japanese then Hindus then Portuguese then Filipinos then, for a time, braceros. Today mostly workers of Filipino and Mexican descent cut the asparagus although a considerable number of Middle Easterners are hiring on. Contracts, though verbal, are renegotiated each year. Growers and laborers have an understanding about the work which is to be done and the conditions under which it is to be accomplished. In the meantime work continues on the development of a mechanical harvester. Technologists have yet to find a replacement for the skilled hands of the experienced Filipino.

There you have it. A brief history of one of the world's most desirous vegetables. There is ever so much more that could be written. You could learn how the Arabs sprinkled asparagus with spices to stimulate the senses; of Brillat-Savarin who told of dreams being provoked by this "lightly exciting" food; of architecture designed in the style of an asparagus spear; of Julius Caesar preferring it with butter; of Egyptians offering it to their gods; of Monet, the French impressionist, who used asparagus as a subject; of the recipe found in the ruins of Pompeii; of the German restaurant in the Black Forest which features 26 asparagus entrées; of. . .the English gentlewoman who broke off her engagement to a gentleman who had thrown "himself at the stuff" at her dinner party. One of the servants had to comb the melted butter out of his hair; of. . .no more. You have been amply advised. Just restrain yourself as you seat yourself before a dish of tender, crunchy, aromatic, steaming asparagus.

James Shebl
Stockton, California

ABOUT STOCKTON
AND THE
ASPARAGUS FESTIVAL

About Stockton & the Asparagus Festival

A view of Stockton was something to be remembered.
There, in the heart of California . . . in the midst of tule
marshes, I found a town . . . and a port.
Bayard Taylor, *Adventures In El Dorado*, 1850

The heartland city called Stockton began with the vision of Charles M. Weber—a German emigrant—man of commerce, fiercely determined to build an agricultural center.

After crossing the plains in 1841 with the famed Bidwell-Bartleson party, Weber quickly came to understand the wonders of California's great Central Valley. This land, stretching between the magnificent Sierra Nevada and Coast ranges and nourished by four major rivers, Weber recognized as the promise of agricultural plenty. The extraordinary rich soil and temperate climate supported his belief that the land was for farming. He soon negotiated for the purchase of the Spanish Land Grant El Rancho Campo de los Franceses—well over 48,000 acres.

Yet it was gold, not wheat, that enabled Weber to permanently settle what was to become the city of Stockton. No matter. The industrious builder understood the need for a supply depot to the southern mines of California's famed gold country—the Mother Lode. He lent his genius to commerce knowing that the land would be developed, though later than he originally thought. He also knew that his agricultural community would require a strong center through which farmers and ranchers could sell and purchase. A wisely built town, founded on thoughtful planning principles and a solid economic base would provide such a center.

Known at first as "Weber's Settlement," occasionally "Castoria," then "Tuleberg"—acknowledging the vast tule islands in the delta formed by the meeting of the Sacramento and San Joaquin River systems—Stockton was named in recognition of Commodore Robert F. Stockton, the military commander of California. The city received its charter July 23, 1850.

Both going and coming, argonauts from around the world passed through Stockton. Local trade increased rapidly and businesses and neighborhoods grew into respectability. Adobe and brush construction became wood and canvas which became brick—to a point at which Stockton became known as "Brick City."

Quickly the city took on its character as a thriving community. Tools were produced for the mines; the wagon and carriage trade enlarged to serve industry and agriculture. The countryside produced the increasingly bountiful harvests which Weber foresaw. Local demands were easily met. Farmers and traders looked for a greater marketplace.

With the coming of the Central Pacific Railroad, the scarcity of easily found surface gold and the advent of hard-rock mining, Stockton turned to agriculture and the manufacture of heavy equipment. This is where the market was.

Wheat fields, legendary in size, surrounded the evergrowing city. With new markets being opened by the railroad, families came to live. Tremendous crops of grain brought great prices. The city grew quickly; it grew solidly. It became known internationally for its produce and products. Sperry's flour, "pure as the drifted snow," was but one of the great brand names to come from Stockton.

Agriculture diversified as farmers developed smaller parcels of land. Reclamation efforts, which began with the building of delta lands levees in the late 1860s, continue through this day. Nearly 500,000 acres are under cultivation. Almost half is below sea level!

Gigantic long-boom dredges were manufactured in Stockton as was the clamshell bucket. In some instances, 200 foot booms swung buckets carrying eight yards of earth! With the levees stabilized, navigable rivers and sloughs became accessible; what was swampland became a garden. The peatlands—virtually an organic compost bowl—today provide extraordinarily fertile ground guaranteeing world class produce and productivity.

Transportation facilities have been continuously improved from the earliest days. By 1933, Stockton became a deep-water port and shipping center. Deepened river channels and sophisticated wharves assure the continuation of world shipping activity.

Shipbuilding, an obvious opportunity for an inland seaport, began in earnest in the 1870s. Though it peaked in World War II when Stockton gained national status for its war effort, shipbuilding continues. Stockton is still known as the source of design and manufacture of world-class pleasure boats.

With over 1,000 miles of waterways formed and secured by the levee system, Stockton is a home marina for thousands of recreational boaters. Beautiful islands teem with wildlife, dazzling plants, and wild flowers.

As Stockton's international reputation for trade and industry grew, local factories furnished farmers around the world with such as plows, harvesters, and thrashers. The environment was ready for local genius. In 1904, Benjamin Holt successfully tested his track-laying tractor—what was to become known as the Holt Caterpillar tractor. It revolutionized earth-moving.

Mining, railroading, and farming also enriched the city of Stockton by increasing its ethnic diversity. From the first, Chinese settled in this community; then the Japanese; the Italians; the Germans; the Mexicans; the Filipinos; the Swedes; the Indians; the Sikhs; the Greeks. The community is an international slice of life. Annual festivals continue old country traditions. Neighborhoods reflect this heritage.

Today, Stockton is a city of over 180,000 people. The metropolitan area has a population of over 418,000. As the county seat of San Joaquin County, Stockton is a political as well as a commercial center. The community is served by three major railways and three short line railroads. Its deep water port serves the world with modern facilities handling dry and liquid bulk commodities, and general cargo including containers. Four airlines service the community, and over 300 manufacturing firms are in the immediate area.

Stockton has a Cultural Heritage Board, Fine Arts Commission, Ballet, Symphony, Civic Theatre, numerous chorale groups, galleries, and the marvelous Haggin Museum.

California's first chartered institution of higher learning, the University of the Pacific, offers a wide range of degree programs. San Joaquin Delta College offers an academic program and occupational programs as does Humphreys College. The University of San Francisco and California State University, Stanislaus and Sacramento campuses, offer classes in Stockton as well.

Stockton's climate is temperate—warm and dry in the summer with relatively cool nights, fanned by the easterly breezes off the Delta waters. Winter is mild with relatively light rains.

The city retains its personality as a thriving community. It recognizes and appreciates its rich cultural heritage; it moves in international circles with ease.

About the Asparagus Festival

STOCKTON, CALIFORNIA is steaming with Asparagus Spear-it! Every year the City of Stockton celebrates the annual asparagus harvest with the Stockton Asparagus Festival. The Asparagus Festival is a two-day community wide event, held the last weekend of April.

The Asparagus Festival has grown from the tiny seed of an idea into an enormous crop of committee chairmen, volunteers (over 1,500), sponsors, non-profit and commercial organizations, all of which work together to harvest the annual festival. The event was an incredible success in 1986 and it continues to get bigger and better.

The Stockton Asparagus Festival was conceived to provide a means to support community projects, charitable groups and service organizations as well as to promote tourism and a positive image to and for Stockton and San Joaquin County. These goals can only be accomplished with the help of a strong and supportive volunteer group. A portion of Festival funds designated for distribution to "charity" is only distributed to those groups who have directly participated in the event through commitment of time and labor. Awards are made on the basis of relative levels on such involvement. Disbursements are made to the individual groups' charity of choice.

The festivities are held in the beautiful Oak Grove Regional Park setting. Highlighting the Festival is the big top tent structure dubbed "Asparagus Alley" where six official gourmet asparagus dishes are prepared for the delight of the Festival-goers. These recipes can be found in this cookbook.

Additional activities include:

- Asparagus memorabilia and history
- Over 150 non-profit and commercial booths including Festival related items, food, arts and crafts
- Continuous entertainment on three stages, featuring a variety of performances including the sounds of Country, Big Band Swing
- Children's entertainment
- Children's Hands on Arts Workshop
- World famous Grupe Belgian Horses
- Asparagus 3-Mile Run
- Hot air balloon rides

12

- Strolling musical and entertainment groups
- Modular tent housing "Wines of the Valley" where many of the area wineries pour premium wines
- Concours d'Elegance featuring some 200 classic and vintage cars

Related activities include:

- Recipe contest
- Cook-off

The Festival is sponsored by the Stockton San Joaquin Convention and Visitors Bureau and is under the direction of Joe Travale, Executive Director. Travale sees the Stockton Asparagus Festival as not only a celebration of the annual asparagus harvest, but as a vehicle to raise community pride and spirit. Travale explains, "After attending numerous other community events throughout California, I am convinced that Stockton is a perfect location for our own major fundraising event. What a better theme than the Asparagus Festival! After all, we are the asparagus capital of the world!"

TIPS

15

SELECTION

QUALITY CHARACTERISTICS OF ASPARAGUS
Firm, straight stalks
Rich green color
Closed, compact tips
Uniformly sized for cooking uniformity
Product is crisp, not wilted

STORAGE

FRESH
Asparagus may be cleaned by washing.
Pat dry and place in plastic bag until ready to use.

FROZEN
Keep frozen asparagus in freezer until ready to use.
Do not defrost before cooking.
Should asparagus become defrosted, cook immediately and do not refreeze!
For best quality, use within eight months.

CANNED
Store canned asparagus in as cool and as dry a place as possible.
For best quality, use within one year.

PROCESSING

FREEZING

Wash thoroughly.
Trim off tough ends.
Wash again if necessary.
Leave spears whole or cut into 2-inch lengths.
Sort according to stalk thickness.
Scald in boiling water for 3 minutes.
Plunge immediately into ice water to stop cooking process.
Drain well.

PROCESS I:

Pack in moisture-proof containers.
Seal, label and freeze.

PROCESS II:

*Place spears or pieces on cookie sheet, separated from
each other.*
Freeze.
*When frozen, place desired number of spears or pieces in plastic
bags for serving sizes, working quickly so asparagus does not
thaw.*
Store in freezer.

CANNING

Recommendation of United States Department
of Agriculture:

Wash and drain asparagus spears, trimming off tough ends.
Leave as spears or cut into pieces.
Boil 3 minutes.
Place hot, into hot canning jars, leaving 1-inch head space.
*Add ½ teaspoon salt to pints, 1 teaspoon salt to quarts, if
desired.*
Cover with boiling water, leaving 1-inch head space.
Adjust caps.
*Process in steam pressure canner 25 minutes for pints, 30
minutes for quarts at 10 pounds pressure (240°F).*

PREPARATION

One basic rule for cooked asparagus is, **NEVER OVERCOOK!** *Cooked asparagus should have a bright green color, and should be tender-crisp, never mushy or watery!*

FRESH

Wash asparagus well.

Break or cut spear at tender part, reserving trimmed ends for purée, soups or salads.

BOILING

Cook quickly in water with or without salt in skillet until tender-crisp.

STEAMING

Tie bundles of asparagus together and place in steamer or bottom of double-boiler with enough boiling water to cover lower half of spears. Cover. Cook until tender-crisp.

MICROWAVING

Place one pound asparagus in a baking dish with tips to center.

Add about ¼ cup water and cover.

Microwave at 100% power for 6-9 minutes for spears, 5-7 minutes for pieces.

Stir or rearrange after half the time.

STIR-FRYING

Stir-fry asparagus pieces in small amount of hot oil or butter.

Stir constantly until tender-crisp.

FROZEN

BOILING

Cook quickly in water with or without salt in skillet until tender-crisp.

MICROWAVING

Place asparagus in a covered baking dish with 2 tablespoons water.

Microwave at 100% power 4-7 minutes. Stir or rearrange once.

CANNED

HEATING

Place contents of can in saucepan.

Heat only until heated through.

MICROWAVING

Place drained, canned asparagus in a covered baking dish with 1 tablespoon liquid.

Microwave at 100% power 2-4 minutes.

Stir or rearrange once.

COLD

Drain well.

Use as appetizer with sauce or use on salads.

COOKING ENDS

Peel ends if necessary.

Place in covered saucepan with water to cover and boil until tender.

Drain and cool.

Strain through sieve or food mill, forcing some of the pulp through, or process in food processor or blender.

Use purée in recipes calling for purée, or mixed with the cooking water for soups, stews, creamed dishes or sauces.

SERVING SUGGESTIONS

Delicious by itself or combine with seasonings, sauces and in dishes.

When cooking, add garlic or onion to the water for additional flavor.

Add chives, parsley, chervil, savory, tarragon or other spices to melted butter poured over asparagus.

Sour cream, yogurt and mayonnaise are easy toppings.

Sauce and dressing recipes are found under that heading in this book.

WINE ACCOMPANIMENTS

Medium dry white wines are good—

Chenin Blanc

Fume Blanc

French Colombards

Of course, consider which wines will go well with your entrée also.

NUTRIENT VALUES IN ASPARAGUS

Asparagus is low in salt, so it is ideal for a low-sodium diet.

Asparagus is very low in calories. There are only four calories per spear, or 66 calories per pound. Great for the weight watcher!

3½ ounces of boiled and drained asparagus contains:

93.6	g.	water
2.2	g.	protein
1.0	mg.	sodium
.6	mg.	iron
183.0	mg.	potassium
20.0	mg.	magnesium
.2	g.	fat
3.6	g.	carbohydrate
.7	g.	fiber
· .4	g.	ash
21.0	mg.	calcium
50.0	mg.	phosphorus
900	Int.	Units Vitamin A
.16	mg.	thiamine
.18	mg.	riboflavin
1.4	mg.	niacin
26.0	mg.	Vitamin C

Asparagus is outstanding as a source of rutin, important for keeping the capillary walls pliable.

One cup of asparagus will provide an adult with:
¾ daily recommended allowance of Vitamin C
⅓ daily recommended allowance of Vitamin A
1/10 daily recommended allowance of Iron

APPROXIMATE PORTIONS

One pound of asparagus serves from two to four people, depending on their appetite for asparagus!

Approximate Number of Spears in One Pound of Asparagus

Colossal Size	7 or less	stalks not less than $^{16}/_{16}"$ in diameter
Jumbo	7 -10	stalks not less than $^{13}/_{16}"$ in diameter
Large	11-20	stalks not less than $^{7}/_{16}"$ in diameter
Standard	21-30	stalks not less than $^{5}/_{16}"$ in diameter
Small	31-45	stalks not less than $^{3}/_{16}"$ in diameter

Diameter is measured from tip down 9"

FRESH ASPARAGUS

1 pound, trimmed . . . . 2 cups, cut up

1 pound, trimmed . . . . . . four ½-cup servings, cooked

1-1½ pounds . . . . 1 pint, frozen

2½-4 pounds . . . . 1 quart, canned

2 cups, chopped . . . . 1 cup purée

PROCESSED ASPARAGUS

1 quart, frozen . . . . 2 cups, grated

1 10-ounce package . . . . 1¼ cups, cut-up

1 14-ounce can . . . . 1⅓ cups, cut-up

ASPARAGUS ALLEY

Asparagus Alley will be the focal point of the Stockton Asparagus Festival. The Alley, will feature six gourmet asparagus dishes which will be prepared under two big-top tents. The dishes were selected from among the favorite asparagus recipes in the San Joaquin Delta area, California's asparagus capital.

Tempting the palate of food fanciers will be **ASPARAGUS BISQUE,** the rich creamy soup topped with sour cream and croutons; **ASPARAGUS PASTA,** a fusilli pasta mixed with asparagus tips and covered with a sautéed vegetable sauce; **ASPARAGUS and SHRIMP SALAD,** a blend of the delicate tips of asparagus and shrimp; **BEEF and ASPARAGUS SANDWICH,** a whole asparagus stalk with slices of specially prepared "beef in a barrel" served on a fresh, warm, Genova roll; **DEEP FRIED ASPARAGUS,** asparagus prepared in a special batter prepared expressly for the Stockton Asparagus Festival. The Asparagus Alley menu is topped off by the simple delight of **FRESH STEAMED ASPARAGUS,** prepared to perfection and topped with a choice of three dressings.

More than 300 volunteers, representing 10,000 man hours are involved in Asparagus Alley. As much thought and work is incorporated in the presentation of the dishes as is given to the preparation. Asparagus Alley, a Gourmet's delight, al fresco, in the beautiful surroundings of Oak Grove Regional Park.

All Recipes in this section have been
formulated and shared by Michael Madden
Asparagus Alley Chairman
1986 Stockton Asparagus Festival

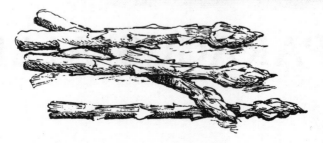

Deep Fried Asparagus

½ cup cornstarch
¾ cup flour
1 tsp. salt
¼ tsp. black pepper
½ tsp. white pepper
½ tsp. celery salt
½ tsp. baking soda
1 tsp. baking powder
2 egg whites
⅔ cup cold flat beer
3 lbs. (2 cups) raw, whole asparagus, cleaned and cut above white end

Mix all ingredients except asparagus in a bowl with a wire whisk until well blended. Dip asparagus individually in the batter and deep fry them in at least 2-inches of peanut oil for 2 minutes or until golden brown.

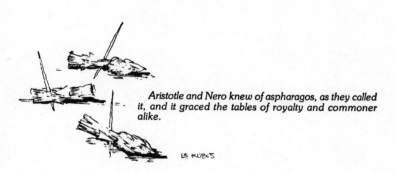

Aristotle and Nero knew of aspharagos, as they called it, and it graced the tables of royalty and commoner alike.

B. KOBUS

Asparagus Bisque

    1 cube butter
    ¾ cup flour
    2 quarts whole milk
    1 cup chicken stock (made from bouillion cube)
    1 tsp. white pepper
    1 tsp. salt
    1 bay leaf
    3 cups cleaned and cooked asparagus, tips and
      center cuts only, (cut into ½-inch pieces)
      instant potatoes (use to thicken bisque if needed)

Roux: In stockpot, melt butter, add flour stirring constantly so mixture doesn't burn. Add 1 quart milk slowly to roux mixture, stirring constantly. When combined and thickened, add remaining milk and chicken stock. Add bay leaf, white pepper and salt. Add asparagus, cook soup slowly for 1 hour.

To serve, top bisque with large sourdough croutons, and a spoonful of sour cream, then sprinkle with dill weed. Makes 1 gallon.

Asparagus and Shrimp Salad

1 lb. cooked and peeled salad shrimp
1 lb. asparagus tips (cooked to tender)
½ cup chopped pimentos
¼ cup finely chopped parsley
½ tsp. white pepper
½ tsp. celery seed
1 tsp. salt
1 Tbsp. horseradish
1 cup mayonnaise
¼ cup fresh squeezed lemon juice
2 hard-boiled eggs, diced

Blend shrimp, asparagus, parsley, pimentos, lemon juice, spices, mayonnaise and horseradish. To serve, place salad on leaf of endive or green leaf lettuce. Garnish with a lemon wedge. Top with diced egg. Serves 4.

Asparagus, a genus of the Liliaceae, or lily family, has some 150 species, both ornamental and edible. The lily family includes such plants as onions, garlic, leeks, lilies, tulips, hyacinths and gladioli.

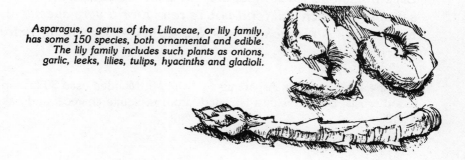

Beef in a Barrel
(Asparagus stacked with very thin slices of beef)

Actually the idea of "Beef in a Barrel" came to me from a restaurant in Walnut Grove called Guisti's. The owner, Mark Morias, prepares beef this way for special parties. It's rather simple.

Cut out an 18" x 18" square on one side at the base of a 55 gallon drum with top removed.

Start a fire* outside the barrel in front of the cut square in the fire ring (Note illustration). A draft will start up through the barrel (like a chimney flue). A crossbar at the top of the barrel is then used to suspend the meat.* The heat from the flue system cooks the meat. A lid on the top of the barrel regulates the amount of heat desired.

—Lid is used only to regulate the temperature

Season the beef with lots of garlic, salt and pepper. Cook beef to internal temperature of 135°.

Slice thinly and stack meat around steamed asparagus stalks, serve in a french roll, and you're ready for a very succulent, tasty treat. Not smoked, not barbequed—Something extra special!

*For the 1986 Stockton Asparagus Festival, Mr. Madden used 30 lbs. top round roasts, cooked with a fire made from mesquite charcoal and oak wood.

TIPS

- Any type of meat may be used—chicken, pork, lamb, etc.
- One pound raw meat yields approximately 12 ounces cooked meat.
- Allow appoximately 18 minutes cooking time per pound of meat.
- Other types of charcoal and wood may be used for the fire.

Asparagus Pasta

⅓ cup olive oil
1 cup sliced fresh mushrooms
½ cup chopped green onions
4 cloves garlic, minced
½ cup olive wedges
1 cup diced tomatoes (fresh or canned, drained)
2 cups cooked asparagus, tips and center cuts only
1½ cups chicken stock
½ cup marsala wine
    cornstarch wash (equal amounts cornstarch and water)
1 Tbsp. Italian seasoning
1 Tbsp. salt
1 tsp. pepper
16 oz. pasta fusilli
    Romano grated cheese

In a large skillet, over high heat, sauté the mushrooms, green onion and garlic in the olive oil until tender. Add the olives and tomatoes. Heat thoroughly. Add cooked asparagus and dry spices, stirring constantly. Add marsala wine to flash point, then add chicken stock. Add cornstarch wash to thicken. Pour over cooked pasta, mix, sprinkle with Romano grated cheese and serve hot.

CALIFORNIA ASPARAGUS GROWERS ASSOCIATION

California Asparagus Growers' Association

As quoted from the minutes, "The first meeting of the incorporators and members of the California Asparagus Growers' Association was held on the 21st day of December, 1921, at 2:15 o'clock P.M., in Brown's Hall, at Walnut Grove, Sacramento County, California."

W.I. Hechtman, Sr. was designated and acted as chairman of the meeting. He called the meeting to order, "...and announced that the seven incorporators had filed Articles of Incorporation with the Secretary of State of California and that the Secretary of State had issued a Certificate of Incorporation to said corporation on the 15th day of December, 1921."

The seven incorporators were: W.I. Hechtman, Sr.; George Peltier; W.C. Kesner; Thomas McCormack; J.M. Gardiner; John S. Brown; George Richardson.

The first elected officers were W.C. Kesner, President; J.M. Gardiner, Vice President; John S. Brown, Treasurer; and Donald McClain, Secretary.

Since the majority of the asparagus acreage was located in the Walnut Grove - Sacramento area, the first office was located in Walnut Grove. As the plantings moved into San Joaquin County, the office was moved to Stockton, presently located at 1850 West Charter Way. San Joaquin County is currently the county in the United States with the largest asparagus production.

The California Asparagus Growers' Association is a non-profit organization of growers of asparagus for commercial purposes. The Association represents the majority of the acreage and production in the San Joaquin Delta - Sacramento Area and assists members in many areas including legislation, research and market development. The main objective of the Association is the orderly marketing of its members fresh market and processed asparagus.

The recipes in this section have been contributed by the members and wives of the 1985 Board of Directors.

"Everyone asks me for this recipe - it is versatile as it can be used as a side dish or cut small into bite-sized appetizers."

Asparagus Torta

3-4 cups fresh asparagus, chopped
1 medium onion, chopped
¼ cup chopped parsley
1 cup whole wheat flour (white can be used)
1 cup grated parmesan cheese
4 eggs
2 Tbsp. water
½ cup olive or salad oil
    salt and pepper to taste

Combine asparagus, onion, parsley, flour and cheese. Beat together eggs, water, oil, salt and pepper. Pour egg mixture into asparagus mixture and combine. Spread mixture into 9x13 baking dish. Bake at 350° for approximately 45 minutes. Serve warm or at room temperature. Serves as many as 18 cut in squares as a side dish, or approximately 100 bite-sized appetizers, depending on size cut.

Julie Abate
(Mrs. Gary Abate)

"Bert and I cook about 30 pounds of asparagus using this recipe for the local golf tournament every year. They are really a big hit!"

Bella Asparagus

2 lbs. large asparagus spears, trimmed and cleaned
½ cup olive oil
3 tsp. wine vinegar
¼ tsp. garlic powder
1 tsp. parsley flakes
   salt and pepper
6 hard boiled eggs, chopped
6 Tbsp. bacon bits

Steam asparagus until tender-crisp and drain. Make dressing with oil, vinegar, garlic powder, parsley flakes, salt and pepper. While asparagus is hot, layer half the spears in a deep dish. Sprinkle half the chopped eggs and bacon bits over the asparagus and half the dressing. Make a second layer of asparagus spears. Top with the remaining chopped eggs, bacon bits and dressing. Serve at room temperature or chill. Serves 4-6.

Gloria Bacchetti
(Mrs. Bert Bacchetti)

"Of all the ways I have had asparagus, this is absolutely my favorite!"

Fried Asparagus

Asparagus, cleaned and trimmed - if small, leave
whole; if large, cut in half lengthwise
salt and pepper
flour
eggs
salt, pepper and garlic powder to taste
corn oil

*Prepare asparagus; sprinkle with salt and pepper. Dip asparagus
in flour to coat. Whip eggs with salt, pepper and garlic powder.
Coat floured asparagus with egg mixture. Fry immediately in
hot corn oil until brown. Serve immediately.*

Mr. Ted Del Carlo

*The San Joaquin Delta District
is the largest asparagus producing county in the
United States.*

*"My friends and family really go for Asparagus & Regal Rice —
it compliments any meal."*

Asparagus and Regal Rice

    2 lbs. fresh asparagus, cleaned and trimmed
    4 cups cooked rice, cooled
    1 tsp. salt
  1-2 dashes ground red pepper
  ½ cup sour cream
  ½ cup milk
  1½ cups shredded sharp cheddar cheese

*Cook asparagus only until tender-crisp; drain well. Combine
rice, salt, pepper, sour cream, milk and ¾ cup cheese. Spoon
half of the mixture into a buttered shallow 2½ quart baking dish.
Reserve 4 asparagus spears for garnish; arrange remaining
asparagus on mixture. Spread remaining rice mixture over
asparagus. Sprinkle with remaining cheese. Bake in a 350° oven
for 20 minutes. Garnish with reserved asparagus, then continue
baking 10 minutes or until hot and bubbly. Serves 6.*

Ann Marie Dell Aringa
(Mrs. Jerry Dell Aringa)

"My favorite way of eating asparagus is absolutely plain, served with mayonnaise."

Best Asparagus

Clean and trim asparagus, amount determined by number of servings needed. Place asparagus in skillet with cold water to which a small amount of salt has been added. Bring asparagus to a boil, cooking only until tender-crisp. Drain and serve immediately with mayonnaise.

Denise Jones
(Mrs. Kevin Jones)

"In my opinion, the best way of preparing asparagus is plain and very simple. . ."

Asparagus

Place desired amount of cleaned and trimmed asparagus in pan. Cover with water and boil until tender-crisp. Drain. Serve immediately with melted butter, salt and pepper to taste.

Annalene Morris
(Mrs. Douglas Morris)

"I enjoy cooking in the kitchen, and I especially enjoy fixing Asparagus Tempura for my friends."

Asparagus Tempura

asparagus, cleaned and trimmed, then cut into
1½-inch pieces.
tempura mix
peanut oil

Prepare asparagus, amount determined by number of servings needed. Prepare tempura mix according to instructions. Heat peanut oil to frying temperature. Dip asparagus into tempura batter, then add to oil. Fry until tender-crisp. Drain on paper towels and serve immediately.

Mr. Richard H. Logemann

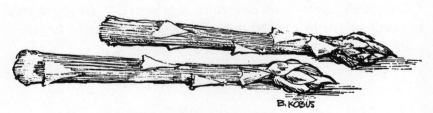

B. KOBUS

*Much of the soil in the San Joaquin Delta District
is peat and will burn when dry.*

"This is a quick 'one dish meal' and it also makes a nice side dish. It can be doubled as many times as necessary."

Asparagus Chicken

    2 tsp. cornstarch
  ¼ tsp. sugar
    1 Tbsp. soy sauce
    2 Tbsp. water
    1 large garlic clove, crushed
    2 Tbsp. oil
    1 whole, boneless chicken breast, partly frozen, then cut crosswise into ¼-inch strips (about 1 cup)
    1 lb. asparagus, cleaned, trimmed, then thinly sliced diagonally (about 2½ cups)

Stir together the cornstarch, sugar, soy sauce, water and garlic. Add the chicken and marinate 1 hour or more. In a black iron skillet over fairly high heat, heat the oil. Add the chicken and marinade, then the asparagus, stir frying 3 minutes or less until chicken is cooked. Serves 2 as a main meal or 4 as a side dish.

Lynn Lyon
(Mrs. William B. Lyon)

"A new baby in our family demands much of my time. This recipe is fast and retains most of the vitamins because of the fast cooking. It can be served as a compliment to any meal, or can be chilled and served as a vegetable salad."

Chinese Asparagus

3 Tbsp. peanut oil
6 pieces ¼-inch sliced ginger root
¼ tsp. salt
1 lb. asparagus, cleaned and trimmed, then sliced in 2-inch diagonal slices
3 Tbsp. chicken stock or water

Heat the oil in a heavy 10-12-inch skillet or wok over high heat. When the oil is almost smoking, add ginger and toss until browned, 2-3 minutes. Remove and discard. Add salt and asparagus to the oil in the pan; cook and toss for 1 minute. Add the stock or water and continue cooking and tossing for 2-3 minutes until the asparagus is tender-crisp. Serves 4.

Judy Mizuno
(Mrs. Clark Mizuno)

"This combination of asparagus, cream sauce and parmesan cheese is hard to beat."

Baked Asparagus with Parmesan Cheese

    2 lbs. asparagus, cleaned and trimmed
      salt
    ¼ cup butter
    2 Tbsp. small bread cubes
    2 Tbsp. flour
    1 cup milk
    1 cup grated parmesan cheese
      salt and pepper to taste
    6 Tbsp. small bread cubes

Cook asparagus in boiling, salted water for 2 minutes. Drain well. Arrange asparagus in the bottom of a 9x9 pyrex baking dish that has been buttered. Melt butter in sauce pan. Add 2 tablespoons small bread cubes, coating well. Blend in flour. Then add milk, cooking until sauce is smooth and thickened. Stir in cheese, salt and pepper to taste. More cheese can be added if desired. Pour sauce over asparagus. Sprinkle with remaining bread cubes. Bake at 350° for 20 minutes. Serves 4.

Nelly Mussi
(Mrs. Rodolfo Mussi)

"This is a popular dish I serve my friends and family. It is great served over steamed rice."

Asparagus with Beef

     1 lb. flank steak, sliced lengthwise 1-inch wide
        then across grain, making bite-sized pieces
     3 Tbsp. oyster sauce
  2½ tsp. cornstarch
    ⅓ tsp. sugar
     1 Tbsp. peanut oil
     1 Tbsp. peanut oil
    ¼ lb. asparagus, cleaned and trimmed, then cut into
        1-inch pieces
    ¼ tsp. salt
     2 Tbsp. water
     1 tsp. peanut oil
     1 8 oz. can bamboo shoots, sliced and drained
  1½ tsp. water
     3 Tbsp. peanut oil
     3 cloves garlic, minced
     4 slices fresh ginger root, unpeeled

Place flank steak in flat pyrex pan. Mix together oyster sauce, cornstarch, sugar and 1 tablespoon peanut oil. Pour mixture over flank steak and marinade for at least ½ hour. Heat 1 tablespoon peanut oil in wok and stir fry asparagus for 5 minutes, adding salt and 2 tablespoons water sprinkled over. Remove from wok and set aside. Heat 1 teaspoon peanut oil in wok and stir fry bamboo shoots for 1 minute, adding 1½ teaspoons water. Remove from wok and set aside. Heat 3 tablespoons peanut oil in wok and stir fry garlic and ginger until slightly brown. Add beef, stir frying for 5 minutes. Add asparagus and bamboo shoots, toss until thoroughly mixed. Serve immediately over rice. Serves 4.

Vicki Mussi
(Mrs. Lory Mussi)

"This is my favorite way of preparing asparagus in a quick method—there's nothing to it after a busy day at work."

Asparagus and Chicken Stir Fry

1 dozen asparagus spears
1 chicken breast (may substitute with pork or beef)
1 tsp. ginger powder
1 Tbsp. soy sauce
2 tsp. sugar
   salt and pepper to taste

Clean asparagus and slice diagonally. Slice chicken into small strips. Sprinkle ginger powder into frying pan. Heat pan. Add chicken strips to pan and sauté until done, stirring constantly. Add asparagus. Sauté until tender-crisp. Add soy sauce, sugar, salt and pepper. Serve immediately with rice. Serves 2.

Nancy Shimasaki
(Mrs. Kyser Shimasaki)

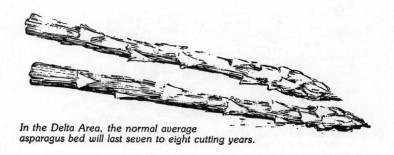

In the Delta Area, the normal average asparagus bed will last seven to eight cutting years.

"With the arrival of Spring and the busy asparagus season, I find myself using quick and easy recipes. The end result— delicious!"

Early Bird Asparagus Supreme

3 lbs. asparagus, cleaned and trimmed, then cooked and drained well
2 cubes butter or margarine
1 package dry onion soup mix
1 cup mozzarella or jack cheese, diced or shredded

Arrange cooked asparagus in 9x13 baking dish. Melt butter. Add soup mix, stirring well. Drizzle mixture over asparagus. Top with cheese. Bake at 450° for 10-12 minutes. Serves 6-8. This recipe is also easy to prepare in the microwave.

Joyce Speckman
(Mrs. Herbert Speckman)

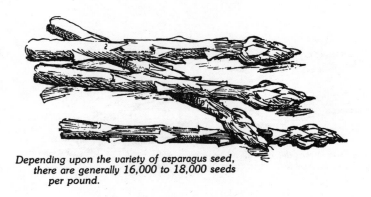

Depending upon the variety of asparagus seed, there are generally 16,000 to 18,000 seeds per pound.

44

"My family thinks this is the best ever way of eating asparagus. As an appetizer or salad, it is most impressive!"

Asparagus Mimosa

3 lbs. asparagus, trimmed and stem ends peeled
Mimosa:
2 hard boiled eggs, sieved
6 sprigs fresh parsley, chopped
1 Tbsp. chopped fresh chives
Dressing:
1½ Tbsp. Dijon mustard
3 Tbsp. wine vinegar
¾ cup vegetable or olive oil
freshly ground pepper and salt to taste

Place asparagus in flat pan, covering with boiling water. Simmer until tender-crisp. Refresh with cold water to stop the cooking process. Drain well, then refrigerate. Make the Mimosa by mixing eggs, parsley and chives. Set aside. Make the dressing by mixing the mustard and vinegar in a bowl, beating with wire whip until smooth. Add oil while beating constantly. Season with salt and pepper to taste. Coat asparagus with dressing. Sprinkle Mimosa over the asparagus tips. Pass any remaining dressing. Serves 6-8.

Pat Zuckerman
(Mrs. Alfred Zuckerman)

APPETIZERS

Deviled Asparagus Cheesewiches

softened butter or margarine
6 slices white bread
2 cans (4½ oz. each) deviled ham
24 asparagus spears, cooked
6 slices american or pimento cheese

Butter one side of each slice of bread and arrange slices, buttered side down on baking sheet. Spread each slice with deviled ham. Top with 4 asparagus spears and cover with slice of cheese. Bake at 400° about 10 minutes. Cut in quarters. Serves 6.

Asparagus Tidbits

3 oz. cream cheese, softened
prepared horseradish to taste
8 slices ham or smoked turkey or dried beef, sliced thinly
8 asparagus spears, cooked

Combine cream cheese with horseradish (to taste). Spread meat slices with this mixture, about 1 teaspoon per slice. Place cooked asparagus spear along one edge of meat slice; roll in jelly-roll fashion. Chill until quite firm. Cut into bite size pieces, securing each with toothpick. Arrange on platter, garnish and serve.

Asparagus Cheese Triangles

        8 oz. cream cheese, softened
        8 oz. cottage cheese
        2 eggs
   1⅓ cups asparagus purée
      30 phyllo leaves (1¼ to 1½ pounds)
        1 lb. butter, melted

Beat eggs and asparagus purée together; mix with cheeses and refrigerate for 1 hour. Place 1 phyllo leaf on a flat surface. Brush with melted butter. Stack 2 or more leaves on top, brushing each with butter. Cut the stack of leaves into 4 lengthwise strips. Place 1 teaspoonful of the cheese mixture at the end of one strip and fold over 1 corner of the strip to make a triangle. Continue to fold over in triangles to the end of the strip.

Brush the triangle with melted butter. Repeat the procedure with the remaining strips of phyllo leaves and filling. Bake in a preheated 500° oven for 20 minutes or until brown. These triangles may be made several hours ahead. Place them on cookie sheets, cover and store in the refrigerator. Makes 40 triangles.

Asparagus Nut Spread

        8 oz. cream cheese, room temperature
      ¼ cup asparagus purée
        2 Tbsp. finely ground pecans

Cream the cream cheese until smooth and soft. Add asparagus purée and pecans and mix well. Serve on crackers or toast.

Asparagus Sticks

  2 Tbsp. water
  ¼ tsp. onion salt
     dash white pepper
  1 beaten egg
  1 lb. asparagus, cooked and drained
  ½ cup fine bread crumbs
  ½ cup butter or margarine

Combine water, onion salt, white pepper and beaten egg. Dip asparagus in egg mixture and coat well. Roll asparagus spears in crumbs and brown in melted butter 6 to 8 minutes. Turn occasionally. Approximately 20 spears.

Asparagus Cheddar Rolls

  6 oz. sharp Cheddar cheese
20 slices bread
  ½ cup soft butter or margarine
  1 Tbsp. chopped parsley
  ½ tsp. dill weed
  3 Tbsp. sliced green onion
     salt and pepper
20 asparagus spears
  ¼ cup melted butter

Cut cheese into sticks about 3 inches long and ½ inch thick. Trim crusts from bread and flatten with rolling pin. Combine ½ cup of butter, parsley, dill, onion, salt and pepper to taste. Spread this mixture evenly on 1 side of each bread slice. Top each slice with asparagus spear and cheese stick. Roll up and secure with toothpick. Place on baking sheet and brush with melted butter. Broil 5 inches from heat until golden brown. Yields 20 rolls.

Garlic Fried Asparagus

    2 lbs. asparagus
    1 cup water
    1 tsp. salt
    ½ tsp. garlic powder
    1 egg
½-¾ cup water
    ½ cup flour
    ½ cup cornstarch
    1 tsp. baking powder

Wash and cut asparagus into 3-inch size or bite size pieces. Parboil about 3-4 minutes in water, salt and garlic powder. Drain and cool. Set aside.

Beat egg and add a little water. Next, add flour, cornstarch and baking powder, and more water to make a medium thin batter. Dip asparagus in batter. Heat oil hot, 350°-375°. Deep fry battered asparagus until light brown. Serves 10-12.

Asparagus Tempura

    2 cups ice water
1⅔ cups all-purpose flour
    1 egg yolk
    ⅛ tsp. baking soda
    3 cups oil
    2 lbs. thin raw asparagus, trimmed
      salt

Combine water, flour, egg yolk and baking soda in medium bowl and beat well until smooth. Cover and refrigerate until ready to use.

To prepare, heat oil in wok or shallow pan to 375°. Dip asparagus in batter and fry in batches until golden brown. Drain on paper towels, salt lightly and serve immediately.

Asparagus Roll-Ups

1 8 oz. package cream cheese, softened
4 Tbsp. margarine or butter, softened
½ tsp. onion powder
⅛ tsp. garlic powder
⅛ tsp. salt
2 tsp. Worcestershire sauce
6 slices bacon, fried and crumbled
20 slices white bread (crust removed)
20 spears asparagus, cooked and trimmed to width
of bread
grated parmesan cheese
Paprika

Blend together cream cheese and margarine. Add onion powder, garlic powder, salt, Worcestershire sauce and bacon. Flatten each piece of bread with a rolling pin. Spread thin coat of cheese mixture on each slice (reserve ½ cup cheese mixture to frost roll-ups). Sprinkle each slice of bread with Parmesan cheese. Add an asparagus spear. Roll up bread; place seam side down on baking sheet, frost tops with reserved cheese mixture, sprinkle with Parmesan cheese and paprika. Cut each roll in ½ or ⅓ rounds. Bake at 400° for 15 minutes or until golden in color.

Asparagus Frittata

  2 yellow onions, chopped
  2 cloves garlic, minced
1½ lbs. cooked asparagus, cut into 1-inch pieces
  1 cup dry bread crumbs
1½ cups grated parmesan cheese
1¼ cups olive oil
  1 cup chopped fresh parsley
1½ tsp. Italian seasoning
  2 tsp. salt
  2 tsp. pepper
 10 large eggs

Sauté onions and garlic in olive oil until tender. Add asparagus, bread crumbs, cheese, parsley, Italian seasoning, salt and pepper and cook together a bit. Beat eggs and add to mixture. Pour into 9x13 pan. Bake at 350° for 40 minutes. May be served either hot or cold. Cut into small squares. This may be frozen.

The Greeks apparently collected asparagus only from the wild, since they gave no directions for cultivating it. The Romans, however, as early as 200 B.C. gave detailed gardening instructions that would be considered good today.

Overnite Marinated Asparagus

1½ lbs. asparagus, cut in bite-size pieces
⅓ cup warm water
 1 Tbsp. sugar (dissolve in water)
½ tsp. dill weed
½ tsp. salt
½ cup oil
½ cup white wine vinegar
 2 Tbsp. grated onion

Blanch asparagus. Drain well. Combine water, sugar, dill, salt, oil, wine vinegar and onion. Cover asparagus with marinade overnight. Serve cold. Serves 6.

Asparagus Mushroom Caps

16 large mushrooms, with stems removed
   melted butter
32 large asparagus tips, cooked
   (or 48 medium)
1-2 cups Hollandaise sauce

Place the mushrooms in a shallow baking dish. Lightly coat with melted butter and place under a preheated broiler. Broil 3 minutes on each side, basting with melted butter frequently. Drain mushroom caps well. Place 2 or 3 asparagus tips in each cap. Fill caps with 1 to 2 tablespoons hollandaise sauce and broil for 3 to 5 minutes, until bubbling. Serve immediately. Makes 16 appetizers.

Water Chestnut—Asparagus Mushrooms

16 mushroom caps, half dollar size
3 Tbsp. butter or margarine
4-5 thinly sliced water chestnuts
¼ tsp. prepared horseradish
1 cup asparagus purée
8 bacon slices or ½ cup bacon bits
   black olives

Remove mushroom stems and hollow caps out slightly, saving stems for other uses. Sauté caps flat side down in butter for several minutes. Lay 1 water chestnut slice in bottom of each cap. Add horseradish to asparagus purée and fill cap with mixture. Soft cook slices of bacon, slit each lengthwise and wrap the resulting ribbon of bacon around caps. Secure with half a toothpick if necessary, (or sprinkle tops with bacon bits). Garnish each cap with olive slice. Bake about 15 minutes at 350° on rack over a baking pan. (If you set them directly on the pan, they will be too moist to handle as finger food). Drain and cool briefly on paper towels before serving. Makes 16 appetizers.

Male flowers are conspicuous, female flowers less conspicuous, and are borne on different plants. The fruit is a three-celled berry which becomes red as it matures. Seeds are large, rounded at the back but more or less flattened on one side, and black in color.

SOUPS

Asparagus Soup

¼ cup minced onion
2 Tbsp. butter
1 cup (¼ lb.) thinly sliced asparagus
½ tsp. paprika
3 cups chicken broth
6 Tbsp. whipping cream
2 Tbsp. cornstarch
2 Tbsp. water

Cook onion in butter until onion is soft. Add asparagus and paprika and cook, stirring until asparagus turns bright green. Stir in chicken broth and whipping cream. Heat to boiling. Blend together the cornstarch and water and stir into soup. Cook just until thickened. Season to taste with salt and pepper. Serves 4-6.

Jan's Favorite Asparagus Soup

3 onions, chopped*
1 cube butter
1-2 lbs. asparagus, sliced thin and diagonally cut
1 gallon water
4 beef bouillon cubes
   grated jack or parmesan cheese to garnish

Sauté onions in butter until turning brown. Add water and bouillon cubes, to taste. Add asparagus to soup and cook until barely tender and serve. Garnish with grated jack or parmesan cheese. Serves 6.

*May substitute onion soup mix

Chilled Asparagus Soup

1 lb. fresh asparagus, cut up or 1-10 oz. package
  frozen cut asparagus
1 cup milk
½ tsp. onion salt
¼ tsp. salt
  dash white pepper
1 cup milk
  dairy sour cream (optional)

Cook asparagus and drain well. In blender container combine asparagus, 1 cup milk, onion salt, salt and pepper. Cover and blend until smooth, about 15 seconds. Add remaining milk; cover and blend to mix. Cover and chill at least 3 hours. If desired, top each serving with dollop of sour cream. Serves 4.

Clear Green Soup

4 cups rich chicken or turkey stock
1 cup (¼ lb.) cut-up asparagus
½ cup halved snow peas
2 Tbsp. minced green onion

Bring the stock to a simmer, add the asparagus and cook until tender, about 5 minutes. Add the snow peas and green onion and simmer 2 minutes. Ladle into bowls and serve. Serves 4.

Cream of Asparagus and Celery Soup

2 cups (about 1 lb.) fresh asparagus, chopped
1 cup chopped celery
1/4 tsp. salt
3 1/2 cups chicken broth
3 Tbsp. butter or margarine
3 Tbsp. flour
1/2 tsp. salt
1/8 tsp. white pepper
1/8 tsp. nutmeg
1/2 cup heavy or whipping cream

Place asparagus and celery in saucepan. Add 1/4 teaspoon salt and boiling water to cover. Return water to boiling, cook 3 to 5 minutes. Drain. Place asparagus, celery and 1/4 cup chicken broth in blender container. Cover and blend until smooth.

In small saucepan, over medium heat, melt butter or margarine. Stir in flour, 1/2 teaspoon salt, pepper and nutmeg until smooth. Add cream and stir until thick. Gradually add remaining chicken broth, stirring constantly until smooth. Do not boil. Continue cooking over medium heat, stirring occasionally until slightly thickened. Stir in puréed vegetables. (Can be prepared in advance to this point. Cover and refrigerate overnight.) Heat and serve. Serves 4.

Asparagus Cheese Soup

(For a Crowd)

½ lb. butter
1 cup flour
2 tsp. salt
½ tsp. white pepper
½ tsp. nutmeg
1½ gallons milk
1½ lbs. cheddar cheese, shredded
5 lbs. frozen asparagus, cooked, drained and diced
   (fresh may be used)
½ lb. cheddar cheese, shredded

Melt butter, blend in flour, salt, pepper and nutmeg; cook about 1 minute. Gradually add milk and cook, stirring constantly, until hot and slightly thickened. Turn off heat and stir in 1½ lbs. cheddar cheese until melted; add asparagus. Keep soup hot over hot water. Just before serving sprinkle an additional 1 Tbsp. shredded cheddar cheese over each portion. Makes 35 cups.

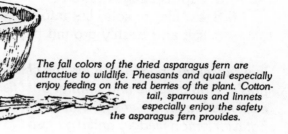

The fall colors of the dried asparagus fern are attractive to wildlife. Pheasants and quail especially enjoy feeding on the red berries of the plant. Cottontail, sparrows and linnets especially enjoy the safety the asparagus fern provides.

Lemon Soup With Asparagus

    3 cups water
    1 envelope chicken rice soup mix
    ¾ lb. asparagus, cleaned, trimmed and cut in 1"
       diagonal pieces
    2 eggs
    3 Tbsp. lemon juice
       minced parsley for garnish (optional)

In medium-size heavy saucepan bring water to boil. Stir in soup mix; cover, simmer 7 minutes. Add asparagus; simmer 3 minutes or until vegetable is crisp-tender.

Meanwhile in small bowl beat eggs with lemon juice until well blended. Beat in about ½ cup hot soup. Remove soup from heat, stir in egg mixture; return soup to medium heat. Stir about 2 minutes or until soup is slightly thickened. Serve hot or chilled, sprinkled with parsley. Serves 4.

Asparagus Sole Soup

    2 cups rich chicken stock
    1 cup asparagus purée
  6-8 oz. filet of sole, cut into pieces
       salt and freshly ground pepper

In a saucepan bring to simmer, the chicken stock and asparagus purée. Add the sole and simmer until fish is opaque and flakes easily with a fork. Season with salt and pepper to taste. Serve hot with lemon wedges and a garnish of minced dill. Serves 3-4.

Yuletime Potato Asparagus Soup

  1 10 oz. package frozen cut asparagus spears
  ⅓ cup chopped onion
  1 Tbsp. margarine or butter
  1 cup water
  1 tsp. instant chicken bouillon
  ¾ cup mashed potato flakes
  1 cup half and half
  1 tsp. chopped fresh dill or ¼ teaspoon dill weed
    dash pepper

Thaw asparagus. In medium saucepan, sauté onion in margarine until tender. Add water and chicken bouillon. Bring to a boil; reduce heat and simmer 5 minutes. Remove from heat; stir in potato flakes until blended. Add asparagus, half and half, dill and pepper. Return to heat; heat thoroughly. Garnish with fresh dill, if desired. Serves 4.

Asparagus is a native of temperate regions and cultivation is most successful where either low temperatures or drought stops growth of the plant and gives it a rest period.

Asparagus and Potato Soup

    2 lbs. fresh asparagus
    3 medium size potatoes
    6 cups boiling water
    1 Tbsp. butter
    2 egg yolks
    ½ cup heavy cream
        salt, pepper, and nutmeg

Clean asparagus. Cook in a very small amount of salted water until almost tender. Remove asparagus from water, and in the same water, cook quartered potatoes until soft. Mash the potatoes in their liquid and add six cups of boiling water and the tender part of the asparagus spears. Reserve six tips for garnish.

Mash the asparagus with a potato masher and stir the soup well. Simmer for about one hour. Put the soup through a strainer and stir in butter.

Just before serving, remove from heat and stir in egg yolks, well beaten, and the cream. Heat soup without boiling, stirring constantly. Season to taste with salt and pepper. Serve in cups garnished with asparagus tips and sprinkle with a dash of nutmeg. Serves 6-8.

Asparagus Tomato Soup

1½ cups (¾ lb.) asparagus, cooked
5 cups chicken or beef broth
1 medium onion, chopped
1 carrot, chopped
   dash pepper
2 tsp. chopped parsley
1 tsp. salt
½ tsp. thyme
1 bay leaf
½ tsp. dried basil leaf
2 cups cooked tomatoes
2 Tbsp. melted butter
2 Tbsp. flour

Combine asparagus, broth, onion, carrot, pepper, parsley, salt, thyme, bay leaf, basil and tomatoes. Cover and simmer 30-35 minutes. Press through a sieve. Combine butter and flour; add to soup and cook 10 to 15 minutes longer. Serves 6-8.

The Delta Area asparagus season generally runs from mid-February through June. During this time, the average number of times a field may be cut would be around 70-75, number of cuttings and production depending on the weather.

Swiss Chard-Asparagus Soup

2 14½ oz. cans chicken broth (3½ cups)
2 cups swiss chard or spinach, torn
1 10 oz. package frozen cut asparagus, thawed or
   1 lb. fresh asparagus, cut up
⅓ cup thinly sliced green onion
¼ tsp. dried tarragon, crushed
⅛ tsp. ground coriander
1 cup light cream or milk
2 Tbsp. all-purpose flour
½ tsp. salt
⅛ tsp. white pepper

In saucepan combine broth, swiss chard or spinach, asparagus, green onion, tarragon and coriander. Bring to boiling; reduce heat and cook, covered, for 8 minutes or until asparagus is tender. In blender container or food processor bowl, purée chicken broth mixture, a portion at a time, until smooth. Return to saucepan.

Meanwhile, blend light cream and flour; add to saucepan along with salt and pepper. Cook and stir until slightly thickened and bubbly. Cook and stir 1 to 2 minutes more. Serve hot or cold. Serves 6.

Quick Soup Ideas

When you are hungry for asparagus and you are in a hurry, try some of these "Soup Mates"...

1 can cream of asparagus soup
2 cans cream of chicken soup
3 soup cans of milk

Mix ingredients together and heat thoroughly. Garnish with grated orange peel.

OR

1 can cream of asparagus soup
1 can scotch broth
1½ soup cans water

Mix ingredients together. Heat thoroughly.

OR

1 can cream of asparagus soup
1 can cream of mushroom soup
2 soup cans of milk (or 1 soup can milk, 1 soup can water)

Mix ingredients together and heat thoroughly. Top with watercress.

OR

1 can cream of asparagus soup
1 can cream of chicken soup
½ soup can milk
2 cups asparagus, cooked
½ cup parmesan cheese

In blender (or food processor) process one can soup, ½ can milk. Empty to pan. Repeat. Liquify asparagus in blender. Add to pan. Heat. Add cheese. Allow to melt. Garnish with tablespoon whipped or sour cream and a touch of parsley. Serve piping hot or chilled. Salt to taste.

SALADS

Asparagus Salad with Lemon Dressing

    1 lb. asparagus, cleaned and trimmed
        juice of ½ lemon
    ¼ cup salad oil
    1 tsp. dry mustard
    1 tsp. chopped green onion
        salt and pepper
        lettuce leaves
    4 tomato slices

Steam asparagus until tender. Drain and chill. Combine lemon juice, oil, dry mustard and chopped onion. Pour over cooked asparagus and chill for several hours. Salt and pepper to taste. Serve on lettuce leaves and tomato slices. If desired, garnish with sieved hard-cooked egg yolk and thin lemon slices. Serves 4.

Curried Asparagus-Mushroom Salad

    ½ cup mayonnaise
    2 Tbsp. sour cream
    ¾ tsp. curry powder
    1 tsp. finely minced onion
    ½ tsp. sugar
    1 tsp. lemon juice
    ¼ lb. mushrooms, sliced
    2 cups chilled cooked asparagus cut into 1½-inch
        pieces (about 1-1½ lbs.)
        salt and pepper to taste

Mix mayonnaise, sour cream, curry powder, onion, sugar and lemon juice. Add mushrooms, asparagus, salt and pepper. Toss gently. Garnish with minced parsley, if desired. Serves 4.

Asparagus Vinaigrette

½ cup safflower oil
3 Tbsp. cider vinegar
½ tsp. dry mustard
½ tsp. pepper
2 tsp. honey
¼ tsp. garlic powder
    dash of paprika
    dash of hot pepper sauce
2 lbs. asparagus spears, steamed until crisp-tender
6 cherry tomatoes
2 eggs, hard-cooked, minced
1 lemon rind, coarsely grated

Make vinaigrette sauce by combining oil, vinegar, honey, mustard, pepper, garlic powder, paprika and hot sauce. Pour over asparagus; cover and refrigerate. To serve, garnish each serving with a cherry tomato and 1 tablespoon of the egg. Top with lemon rind. Serves 6.

Backyard Supper Salad

2 cups elbow macaroni
¼ cup bottled Italian salad dressing
⅔ cup mayonnaise
1 tsp. salt
1 Tbsp. fresh chopped chives or 1½ tsp. dry chives
½ tsp. fennel seed (optional)
1 lb. asparagus, cooked and chilled

Boil elbow macaroni in salted water. Drain and chill. Mix together dressing, mayonnaise, salt, chives, fennel seed and macaroni in serving bowl. Garnish top with asparagus spears. Serves 6-8.

Asparagus with Special Dressing

1 lb. asparagus, cut into 2-inch pieces
1 small head lettuce, torn into bite-size pieces
1 cup sliced celery
¼ cup sliced green onions with tops
½ cup salad oil
2 Tbsp. white wine vinegar
2 Tbsp. lemon juice
¼ cup finely chopped, cooked beets
1 egg, hard-cooked, finely chopped
1 Tbsp. chopped parsley
1 tsp. paprika
1 tsp. sugar
1 tsp. salt
½ tsp. dry mustard
4-5 drops bottled hot pepper sauce

Steam asparagus until tender. Drain and chill. Combine with lettuce, celery and onion. Combine remaining ingredients in a jar; cover and shake well. Pour over salad; toss lightly. Serves 6-8.

Left-Over Asparagus Salad

Cut left-over cooked asparagus spears into diagonal strips. Tear lettuce into small pieces. Toss asparagus and lettuce with mayonnaise. Sprinkle with lemon juice and pepper.

Four Vegetable Salad

½ head lettuce
1 lb. fresh asparagus spears, cooked and chilled
6 radish roses
½ pint plain yogurt
1 Tbsp. minced fresh chives
1 Tbsp. bottled salad dressing, any type
1 tsp. sugar
½ tsp. salt

Blend yogurt, chives, salad seasonings, sugar and salt; chill. At serving time, cut lettuce into 6 portions and place on 6 plates. Top with asparagus spears and radish rose. Spoon dressing across each salad. Serves 6.

Asparagus 'N Guacamole

1 lb. asparagus
1 cup peeled and diced fresh tomato
1 Tbsp. chopped onion
½ tsp. salt
⅛ tsp. pepper
1 Tbsp. lemon juice
2 medium ripe avocados, diced
1 Tbsp. mayonnaise
1 tsp. olive oil
½ tsp. Worchestershire sauce

Cook asparagus and chill. Mix all other ingredients together, blend well. Serve over cold, cooked asparagus. Serves 4.

Asparagus with Tarragon Sauce

    2 lbs. fresh asparagus, cooked and chilled
    1 egg yolk
    ¼ cup dairy sour cream
    2 Tbsp. tarragon vinegar
    ½ tsp. dry mustard
    ½ tsp. salt
    3-4 drops hot pepper sauce
    ½ tsp. sugar
    2 tsp. minced fresh parsley
    ½ cup vegetable oil
      lettuce leaves

In blender combine egg yolk, sour cream, vinegar, mustard, salt, pepper sauce, sugar and parsley for 30 seconds. Add vegetable oil very gradually with blender on high speed. Chill. Place asparagus on lettuce leaves and top with sauce. May be used as an appetizer. Serves 6-8.

Asparagus with Fresh Herb Mayonnaise

    1½ cups mayonnaise
    1 tsp. prepared mustard
      dash cayenne
    2 Tbsp. minced fresh parsley
    2 Tbsp. minced chives
    1 Tbsp. minced fresh tarragon
    1 Tbsp. minced fresh dill
    2 lbs. asparagus, cooked and chilled
    4 eggs, hard-cooked, quartered
      lettuce leaves

Mix mayonnaise and herbs. Refrigerate several hours to allow flavors to blend. Divide asparagus into four bunches. Place on lettuce leaves on four individual serving dishes. Surround with eggs and spoon mayonnaise over all. Serves 4.

Asparagus-Pimento Vinaigrette Salad

2 lbs. asparagus
½ cup salad oil
¼ cup wine vinegar
1 tsp. dry mustard
1 tsp. salt
¼ tsp. pepper
1 tsp. sugar
¼ tsp. paprika
   lettuce leaves
   pimento

Wash and trim asparagus. Steam until tender. Drain and chill. Mix oil, vinegar, mustard, salt, pepper, sugar and paprika. Pour over asparagus in a shallow non-metal dish. Marinate overnight in refrigerator. To serve, remove asparagus from marinade with a slotted spoon and arrange on lettuce leaves in a shallow serving dish. Garnish with pimento. Serves 6.

Asparagus Sour Cream Salad

For each serving use:
½ cup asparagus, cooked, cooled and chopped
2 tsp. sour cream
2 tsp. almond slices or chopped cashews
   lettuce leaves

Combine all ingredients and serve on lettuce leaves. This recipe can be made in whatever quantity you wish, depending on your need.

Hot Bacon and Asparagus Salad

  6 slices bacon
½ cup chopped almonds
  1 lb. asparagus, fresh or frozen
  6 Tbsp. vinegar
  1 Tbsp. sugar
½ tsp. dry mustard
⅛ tsp. pepper
  1 quart torn, mixed salad greens
  2 eggs, hard-cooked, sliced

Dice bacon and fry in skillet until crisp and browned; remove from pan and drain. Take 3 tablespoons of the bacon fat and add almonds. Sauté until roasted a golden color. Remove and set aside.

Trim asparagus and cut on sharp diagonal to get pieces about 1½-inch long. Add asparagus to skillet, cover and cook over medium-high heat for about 5 minutes, shaking pan or stirring often to prevent sticking. When asparagus is tender-crisp, add vinegar, sugar, mustard, pepper and crisp bacon to pan; heat 1-2 minutes, stirring.

Put greens in salad bowl; pour asparagus mixture over and top with sliced eggs. Sprinkle with roasted almonds. Toss at table and serve promptly. Serves 4.

Asparagus in Tomato Cups

1 lb. asparagus, cut into 1-inch pieces
1 can (3 oz.) sliced mushrooms, drained, or ½ cup
  sliced fresh mushrooms
¼ cup green onion, sliced
⅓ cup Italian dressing
  dash pepper
1 tsp. chopped parsley
6 medium tomatoes

Steam asparagus until tender. Drain and cool. Add mushrooms, onion, salad dressing, pepper and parsley and toss gently. Chill well. Meanwhile, cut a slice from stem end of each tomato and discard. Scoop out center of tomatoes to make shells about ¼ inch thick. Invert shells; chill. To serve, sprinkle chilled tomato shells with salt and spoon in asparagus mixture. Serves 6.

Asparagus in Avocado Boats

2 large avocados, halved, pulp removed and skins
  reserved
½ cup mayonnaise
  juice of ½ lemon
3 cups (1 lb.) asparagus, cooked and chilled, cut into 1-inch pieces

Purée avocado pulp in blender. In mixing bowl, fold together avocado pulp, mayonnaise and lemon juice with asparagus pieces. Fill avocado skins with mixture and chill. May be garnished with lemon wedges. Serves 4.

Asparagus and Walnut Salad

    1 cup walnut halves
  1/3 cup tamari soy sauce
  1/3 cup sugar
  1/3 cup cider vinegar
    3 Tbsp. walnut oil or safflower oil
1 1/2 lbs. asparagus, steamed, cut to 1-inch pieces and
      kept hot

Roast walnuts in 300° oven 20 minutes; chop coarsely and set aside. In saucepan combine tamari soy sauce, sugar, vinegar and oil and place over low heat, stirring until sugar dissolves. Remove from heat and mix walnuts into dressing. Pour dressing over asparagus and toss lightly; chill. Remove salad from refrigerator 30 minutes before serving. Serves 4.

Asparagus-Shrimp Vinaigrette Salad

  1 lb. asparagus
  1 egg, hard-boiled
  3 green onions, minced
  1 Tbsp. minced parsley
1/4 tsp. salt
    dash pepper
  4 Tbsp. white wine vinegar
1/2 cup salad oil
1/4 lb. tiny shrimp, cooked and shelled
    lettuce leaves

Steam asparagus until tender. Drain and chill. Mash hard-cooked egg and combine with remaining ingredients except lettuce leaves. Arrange lettuce leaves on 6 individual salad plates. Top each plate with 3-4 spears of cold, cooked asparagus. Spoon dressing onto each salad. Serves 6.

Asparagus-Shrimp Salad

    1 lb. fresh or frozen shrimp, shelled and cleaned
1-1½ lbs. fresh asparagus
    1 lemon, thinly sliced
    ¼ cup sliced green onion
    2 Tbsp. minced parsley
    1 recipe fresh herb dressing*
    3 medium tomatoes, peeled and sliced
      lettuce leaves

Cook shrimp, drain and set aside. Cook asparagus until tender. Drain well. Place shrimp, asparagus, lemon slices, onion and parsley in mixing bowl. Pour herb dressing over all, cover and chill well, stirring once or twice. To serve, drain and toss with tomato slices; pile into lettuce-lined bowl. Serves 4.

*Fresh Herb Dressing: Mix ½ cup salad oil, 4 Tbsp. vinegar, ¼ tsp. salt, dash cayenne, ⅛ tsp. pepper, 1 Tbsp. EACH of the following fresh minced herbs: parsley, basil, chervil, oregano.

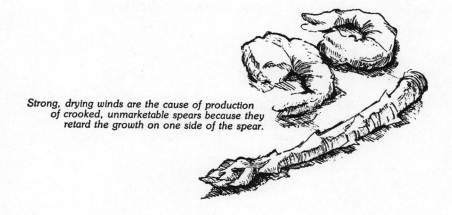

Strong, drying winds are the cause of production of crooked, unmarketable spears because they retard the growth on one side of the spear.

Asparagus Seafood Delight

1 cup asparagus, cut into 1-inch pieces
½ cup chopped celery
1½ cup crabmeat, cut into small pieces
    lettuce leaves

Dressing

1 cup olive oil
¼ cup lemon juice
1 Tbsp. prepared mustard
½ tsp. ground pepper
½ tsp. parsley flakes
¼ cup wine vinegar
1 Tbsp. minced onion
1 tsp. salt
½ tsp. dried chives
½ tsp. dillweed

Place asparagus in saucepan and cover with cold water, bring to a boil for one minute, drain and chill. Mix chilled asparagus with chilled celery and crabmeat. Combine all ingredients for dressing and mix well until blended. Place lettuce leaves on each salad plate. Place ¼ cup salad on each. Pour dressing over salad and serve with lemon wedges. Serves 4.

Spring Antipasto Salad

⅓ cup mayonnaise
½ cup sour cream
2 Tbsp. chopped parsley
1 Tbsp. lemon juice
1 Tbsp. chopped chives
½ tsp. basil
1 cup flaked crab, canned or fresh
4 oz. Monterey jack cheese, cubed (⅔ cup)
1½ cups cooked rice
   lettuce leaves
1 large tomato, sliced
4 oz. cheddar cheese, cut into sticks
2 oz. prosciutto or ham, thinly sliced
½ lb. fresh asparagus, steamed

Combine mayonnaise, sour cream, parsley, lemon juice, chives and basil. Flake crab. Fold crab, cheese cubes and rice into sour cream dressing, chill. Line serving plate with lettuce leaves. Spoon crab salad into center. Garnish with tomato, asparagus and cheese sticks wrapped in ham. Serves 4.

Elegant Asparagus Mold

 2½ lbs. asparagus, (as near same size as possible)
  ½ cup cold water
  2 envelopes unflavored gelatin
  2 Tbsp. butter
  2 Tbsp. flour
  2 cups milk
  1 package (8 oz.) cream cheese
  1 cup heavy cream
  ½ tsp. salt

Steam asparagus until tender. Drain and cool. Trim each spear to 3 inches in length; set aside. Thinly slice remaining asparagus pieces and measure about 2½ cups; set aside. Combine cold water and gelatin and let stand 5 minutes. In a saucepan, melt butter and blend in flour. Gradually add 1 cup milk; cook, stirring until thickened. Blend in dissolved gelatin and stir until blended. Remove from heat.

Whirl cream cheese and the remaining 1 cup milk in blender until smooth. Stir cheese-milk mixture into hot mixture. Chill until slightly cooled. Carefully stir in the 2½ cups sliced asparagus.

Whip the cream until stiff; fold into cooled milk mixture. Chill until the consistency of soft whipped cream, stirring occasionally. Stand the 3-inch pieces of asparagus around the sides of an 8-inch spring form pan with removable sides or bottom (this is important); space tips evenly. Carefully ladle the partially set asparagus mixture into the pan. Chill at least 4 hours or until firmly set.

Dip a towel in hot water, wring out, and wrap around pan sides for 30 seconds. Remove pan sides and leave salad on pan bottom. Cut in wedges to serve. Serves 8-12.

Tangy Salad Mold

2 envelopes unflavored gelatin
1 cup water
2 cans (10¾ oz. each) cream of asparagus soup
1 package (8 oz.) cream cheese, softened
¼ cup lemon juice
2 Tbsp. sugar
  dash of bottled hot pepper sauce
  green food coloring
⅓ cup finely chopped celery
2 Tbsp. finely chopped onion

In a saucepan soften gelatin in water for about 5 minutes. Stir over low heat until gelatin dissolves. Add soup and blend well. Set aside. Beat cream cheese in a small bowl until fluffy. Beat in lemon juice, sugar and hot pepper sauce. Stir in soup mixture gradually. Add a few drops coloring to tint a nice green. Stir in celery and onion. Pour into a lightly oiled 5-cup mold and chill several hours. Unmold on serving plate and garnish with parsley, if desired. Serves 8.

Until recently, it has not proven successful to replant asparagus on land that has been used to grow asparagus due to soil related diseases. With hybrid varieties developed by the University of California, asparagus can now be replanted on soil which was previously planted to asparagus; however, it is recommended that a period of ten years be allowed to pass after the old beds are pulled out.

Asparagus Salad Soufflé

1 package (3 oz.) lime jello
1 cup hot water
½ cup cold water
1½ Tbsp. vinegar
½ cup mayonnaise
    pinch of salt
1 cup asparagus, cooked, cooled and drained
¾ cup cottage cheese
⅓ cup finely chopped celery
1 Tbsp. chopped green onion

Dissolve jello in hot water, add cold water, vinegar, mayonnaise and salt. Blend with electric mixer. Chill until partially set then beat with mixer until fluffy. Add asparagus, cottage cheese, celery and onion and mix well. Chill until firm. Serves 6.

Asparagus Mold Royale

2 10 oz. packages frozen asparagus or 2 lbs. fresh
    asparagus, cooked
1 cup hot liquid (from asparagus)
1 Tbsp. unflavored gelatin, dissolved in ¼ cup
    water
½ cup mayonnaise
½ cup cream, whipped
1 tsp. salt
2 Tbsp. lemon juice
1 cup thinly sliced almonds

Heat asparagus liquid and pour over dissolved gelatin. When partially set, fold in mayonnaise, whipped cream, salt and lemon juice. Add asparagus and almonds. Pour into mold and congeal. Serve with mayonnaise whipped with a little lemon juice. Serves 12.

Asparagus Salad Mold Supreme

1 envelope unflavored gelatin
¼ cup cold water
1 can (10¾ oz.) cream of asparagus soup
1 Tbsp. lemon or lime juice
¼ tsp. salt
1 cup cream-style cottage cheese
⅓ cup sour cream
   green food coloring
1 10 oz. package frozen asparagus or 1 lb. fresh,
   cooked and cut into pieces
⅓ cup finely chopped celery
2 Tbsp. canned pimento, chopped

In saucepan soften gelatin in water for about 5 minutes. Stir over low heat until gelatin dissolves. Blend in soup, juice, salt, cottage cheese and sour cream. Add a few drops of green food coloring to tint a nice green color. Chill until partially set, then fold in asparagus, celery and pimento. Pour into 5-cup mold. Chill until firm. Unmold on serving plate and garnish with parsley or celery leaves, if desired. Serves 5-6.

MAIN
DISHES

Steak and Asparagus

  1 lb. round steak
  1 Tbsp. oil
  1 lb. fresh asparagus
  2 large onions, sliced thickly
¼ cup sherry wine
  1 tsp. cornstarch
  3 Tbsp. Japanese soy sauce
½ tsp. sugar

To tenderize meat, pound to ¼-inch thickness. Puncture meat in several places with fork. Heat oil in nonstick skillet and brown the steak quickly on both sides. It should be very rare, almost raw inside. Remove to cutting board and slice against grain in very thin strips. Set aside.

Slice cleaned asparagus into 1-inch lengths. Thick-slice onions. Combine onions, asparagus and sherry wine in the same skillet. Cover and cook 2 minutes. Separate the onion into rings.

Stir together cornstarch, soy sauce and sugar, add to skillet. Cook and stir until mixture thickens and forms sauce. Stir in sliced steak strips. Cook only until heated through. Meat should be rare, vegetables crunchy-fresh. Serves 4.

Steak and 'Gras

  2 Tbsp. olive oil
3-4 cloves garlic, slivered
  1 large flank or sirloin steak, sliced in ¼-inch slices
  1 Tbsp. soy sauce
  1 yellow onion, diced
  2 stalks celery, diced
½-¾ lb. asparagus, cut into ½-inch diagonal slices
  ½ cup water
1-2 Tbsp. brandy or whiskey
    cornstarch (optional)

Heat large fry pan with olive oil. Add garlic, steak that has been sliced into ¼-inch slices, and soy sauce. Cook until brown. Remove from pan and set aside.

Add onion, celery and sliced asparagus to pan with drippings. Stir-fry 2-3 minutes. Add water and brandy, cover cooking 5 minutes or until 'gras is tender. Return beef and garlic mixture to pan. Stir-fry 1 minute more.

A small amount of cornstarch may be added to thicken juices if desired. May be served over rice or noodles. Serves 4-5.

Sukiyaki

1 lb. sirloin, ½-inch thick, thinly sliced
2 Tbsp. oil
1 cup diagonally sliced celery
1 cup thinly sliced onion
1 clove garlic, finely minced
1 cup sliced mushrooms
1 lb. asparagus, cleaned, trimmed, cooked and
    drained
½ cup water
2 Tbsp. sherry
1 Tbsp. soy sauce
1 Tbsp. cornstarch
1 tsp. salt
1 beef bouillon cube
½ tsp. sugar
¼ tsp. ginger

Heat oil in heavy pan, add celery, onion and garlic. Stir and fry over high heat 1 minute. Add mushrooms, stir and fry. Add cooked asparagus, heat. Blend remaining ingredients together and add to mixture. Cook until sauce thickens. Serve plain or with hot rice. Serves 4.

Asparagus Surprise Casserole

2 lbs. ground beef
1 large onion, chopped
1 tsp. oregano
garlic powder, onion powder, salt and pepper to taste
1 lb. fresh asparagus, cut in 2-inch pieces
½ lb. cheddar cheese, grated
2 cans mushroom soup
2-3 lbs. fresh mashed potatoes

Brown ground beef and onion together, add garlic and onion powders, oregano, salt and pepper. Place in 9x13 casserole dish, layer of meat and layer of asparagus. Sprinkle ½ of grated cheese over asparagus. Add a layer of undiluted mushroom soup, then layer of mashed potatoes. Place rest of the grated cheese on top. Bake at 350° for 35 minutes. Serves 6-8.

Asparagus-Chicken Divan

1 10 oz. package frozen asparagus pieces
6 slices cooked or canned chicken or turkey
1 Tbsp. melted butter or margarine
1 can undiluted condensed cream of chicken soup, heated
½ cup grated processed american cheese

Cook asparagus as label directs. Arrange chicken in 12x8x2 baking dish; top with asparagus and butter. Then combine heated soup and cheese; pour over asparagus. Brown lightly under broiler. Serves 4.

Asparagus Chicken

  2 tsp. cornstarch
  ¼ tsp. sugar
  1 Tbsp. Japanese soy sauce
  2 Tbsp. water
  1 large clove garlic, crushed
  2 Tbsp. oil
  1 boneless skinless chicken breast, halved and partly frozen and then cut crosswise in ¼-inch wide strips (about 1 cup)
  1 lb. medium thick asparagus, thinly sliced diagonally (2 generous cups)

In a shallow bowl stir together cornstarch, sugar, soy sauce, water and garlic. Toss chicken in mixture and marinate for an hour or longer.

In a 10-inch black iron skillet over fairly high heat, heat the oil; add the chicken and its marinade and the asparagus; stir-fry, using a pancake turner to toss and turn mixture. Cook about 3 minutes or less (until chicken loses its translucent look and is cooked through).

Rolled Chicken and Asparagus

2 whole chicken breasts, boned and skinned
24-30 fresh asparagus spears
3 Tbsp. oil and vinegar salad dressing
½ cup chopped green onion
1 tsp. salt
⅛ tsp. pepper
2 Tbsp. sesame seed, lightly toasted

Cut chicken breasts into 8-10 strips, about 1-inch x 6-inch each. Wrap each strip in corkscrew fashion around bundle of 3 uncooked asparagus spears and place in shallow baking dish. Repeat for all strips.

Spoon oil and vinegar dressing over bundles, then sprinkle with onion, salt and pepper. Cover and bake in 350° oven for 15 minutes. Remove cover, sprinkle with sesame seeds and bake about 15 minutes longer or until fork can be inserted in chicken with ease. Serve hot or refrigerate until chilled and serve cold. Serves 4-5, 2 rolls each.

During the winter, after the fern is chopped and the growers flood the fields, water fowl migrate from the flyways to the central valley to raft and feed on the asparagus fields, looking for weed seeds.

Baked Asparagus and Flounder

2 lbs. fresh asparagus
1½ lbs. fresh or frozen thawed flounder fillets
2 Tbsp. butter or margarine
¼ cup chopped onions
2 Tbsp. flour
1¾ cups milk
¼ cup dry white wine
2 tsp. fresh lemon juice
½ tsp. salt
¼ tsp. dill weed
⅛ ground black pepper
2 Tbsp. chopped parsley
2 Tbsp. shredded swiss cheese

Cook cleaned asparagus until tender. Drain. Divide asparagus into 4 portions. Wrap 1 fish fillet around each bundle. Arrange in shallow baking dish. Melt butter in small saucepan. Add onion and cook until tender. Blend in flour smoothly. Add milk all at once; heat, stirring constantly, until mixture thickens, then boil. Remove from heat; stir in wine, lemon juice, ½ tsp. salt, dill, pepper and parsley. Spoon sauce over fish. Sprinkle with cheese. Cover and bake in 350° oven about 30-35 minutes or until fish flakes when tested with fork. Serves 4.

Veal Oscar

6 veal cutlets (¼-inch thick, sirloin cut)
  salt and pepper
  flour and butter
24 warmed asparagus tips, cooked tender
30 crab legs slightly warmed in butter
2-3 Tbsp. beef stock
  Bearnaise sauce

Flatten the cutlets lightly on both sides with a mallet. Season with salt and pepper and dip in the flour. Sauté in butter over brisk heat - turning the cutlets several times until done to golden brown. Do not use too much butter, being careful not to burn the meat. Place on a large warmed platter. On each cutlet place 4 or 5 warmed asparagus tips and on top of the asparagus place 5 or 6 crab legs.

Pour the stock in a skillet in which the cutlets were browned and let cook a few minutes. Pour this over the cutlets and keep the whole platter warm until ready to serve with Bearnaise sauce. Serves 6.

Suggestion: Use Knorr's packaged Bearnaise Sauce

Shrimp and Asparagus Fettuccine

½ cup heavy cream
½ cup milk
1 cup grated white cheese
1 cup grated parmesan cheese
4 egg yolks
1 lb. cooked fresh shrimp
1 lb. cooked asparagus
  dash ground nutmeg
  freshly ground pepper to taste
8 oz. fettuccine noodles, cooked
  lemon slices for garnish

Combine cream, milk and cheeses in top of double boiler placed over simmering water. Cook and stir until cheeses melt; do not boil. Beat in egg yolks, one at a time. Cook and stir until sauce thickens. Add shrimp, asparagus, nutmeg and pepper. Serve over cooked noodles and garnish with lemon slices. Serves 4.

Scalloped Asparagus and Spaghetti

2 oz. spaghetti
1 cup (½ lb.) asparagus, sliced diagonally, cooked
  and drained
1 cup thin white sauce
  salt and pepper to taste
  bread crumbs mixed with small amount of melted
  butter

Cook spaghetti and drain. Place alternate layers of spaghetti and asparagus in greased baking dish. Season white sauce and pour over spaghetti and asparagus. Sprinkle with bread crumbs and bake at 350° until golden brown, about 20 minutes. Serves 2.

Pasta E Asparagi

2 lbs. asparagus, cleaned and trimmed, cut into
   2-3 inch pieces
½ lb. tender green beans (baccicia string beans)
   cleaned, cut into 2-3 inch pieces
¼ cup butter
1¼ lbs. fresh green pasta or 1 lb. dried pasta
10 cups water
2 Tbsp. salt
¼ cup butter
4 Tbsp. olive oil
6 scallions, sliced
1 lb. mushrooms, sliced
2 cloves garlic, minced
   salt and pepper to taste
¼ tsp. nutmeg
¼ cup butter
½ cup cream

Steam asparagus and beans until tender crisp. Toss gently with ¼ cup butter. Cover to keep warm and set aside.
Bring water and salt to boiling. Add pasta and cook to al dente. Drain.

Meanwhile, place ¼ cup butter and olive oil in large frying pan and place over high heat. Add scallions, toss and add mushrooms, tossing carefully and cooking for 5-8 minutes. Add garlic. Lower heat, then add salt, pepper and nutmeg.

In another saucepan, melt ¼ cup butter and mix with cream. Mix well and add to scallion-mushroom mixture, stirring well. Add half of the steamed vegetables and the pasta to the sauce. Toss gently. Serve on hot platter, arranging the remaining vegetables around platter. Serves 8.

Risotto with Asparagus

3 Tbsp. butter
½ medium onion, chopped fine
2 lbs. asparagus, cleaned and trimmed, cut in
  2-inch pieces
1⅔ cups rice
5½-6 cups chicken broth, boiling
  salt to taste
1 tsp. finely chopped parsley
¼ cup grated parmesan cheese
2 Tbsp. butter

Melt butter in heavy saucepan and add chopped onion. Sauté for three minutes, then add asparagus. Continue to stir, cooking for another 2 minutes. Add rice. Continue stirring. Begin pouring boiling chicken broth into mixture, a little at a time, stirring until all broth is used. Cook about 15 minutes or until rice is cooked.

Add salt, parsley, grated cheese and butter. Toss gently and serve immediately. Serves 6-8.

Asparagus and Egg Casserole

1½ lbs. fresh asparagus
1½ cups thin white sauce
5 eggs, hard-cooked
  buttered bread crumbs

Clean asparagus, cut in 1-inch pieces, and cook until tender. Drain, saving liquid. Make white sauce, using evaporated milk diluted with asparagus liquid instead of milk. Fold in the cooked asparagus. Arrange layers of creamed asparagus in buttered casserole with sliced, hard-boiled eggs between layers. Cover with buttered crumbs and bake in a moderately hot oven (400°) until thoroughly heated, about 20 minutes. Serves 5.

Creamed Asparagus

2 lbs. fresh asparagus
1 can cream of asparagus soup
½ cup half and half cream
1 tsp. lemon juice
1 beaten egg
½ cup slivered, blanched and toasted almonds
6 patty shells or toast points

Slice asparagus with long, slanting cuts about ½-inch thick. Cook until just barely tender. Drain. Combine soup, half and half, lemon juice and egg in saucepan and heat thoroughly. Add the asparagus and almonds. Serve in 6 patty shells or over toast points. Serves 6.

Asparagus Newburg

¾ lb. asparagus, cooked and cut in 1-inch pieces
1¼ tsp. salt
9 almonds, blanched and sliced (1½ oz.)
3 Tbsp. butter or margarine
2 Tbsp. flour
½ cup milk
1 cup sliced fresh mushrooms
1 tsp. cooking sherry
toast squares

Sauté almonds in heated butter for a few minutes until golden brown. Do not scorch. Stir in flour until well blended. Add milk gradually. Cook over medium heat until sauce boils and thickens, stirring to keep smooth. Add asparagus, mushrooms and sherry. Blend carefully. Cover and simmer for a few minutes. Stir occasionally. Serve over toast squares. Serves 4.

Poached Eggs with Asparagus and Wine Sauce

     2 Tbsp. butter or margarine
     2 Tbsp. flour
     2 Tbsp. chopped parsley
     1 tsp. grated onion
     ½ tsp. salt
     ¼ tsp. dried tarragon
     ¼ tsp. hot pepper sauce
     1½ cups milk
     2 cups dry white wine
     4 eggs
     2 English muffins, split and toasted
     1 10 oz. package frozen asparagus spears, cooked
        (or 1 lb. fresh)

In medium saucepan melt butter over low heat. Blend in flour, parsley, onion, salt, tarragon and hot pepper sauce. Cook 2-3 minutes, stirring constantly. Gradually stir in milk and cook over medium heat, stirring until mixture thickens and comes to a boil, about 10 minutes. Set aside.

In a 8½-inch omelet skillet, heat wine until it begins to boil. Reduce heat so that wine is simmering. Break eggs one at a time into a saucer or custard cup. Slip eggs gently into simmering wine. Let eggs cook until white is firm. Using slotted spoon, remove eggs, drain well and place them on toasted English muffin halves.

Place muffin halves with eggs and drained asparagus on an oven-proof platter and keep warm in 250° oven while finishing sauce preparation. Add ½ cup of the hot wine used to poach eggs to the sauce mixture. Cook over medium heat, stirring constantly, until mixture is smooth. Pour wine sauce over both eggs and asparagus to serve. Serves 4.

Asparagus Soufflé Roll

```
6 Tbsp. butter or margarine
¾ cup flour (unsifted)
1½ lbs. asparagus tips
1 tsp. dry mustard
½ tsp. salt
3 cups milk
4 eggs, separated
1 cup grated swiss cheese
½ cup milk
```

Line a greased 10x15x1 pan with foil. Grease and flour foil. In large saucepan, melt butter over medium heat. Stir in flour, mustard and salt. Very gradually stir in 3 cups milk. Stir 8-10 minutes until thick. Remove from heat. Set aside 1 cup white sauce. Beat yolks and beat in white sauce. Beat egg whites until stiff and fold into yolk mixture. Pour into pan and bake at 325° for 35-40 minutes or until the center springs back.

Cook asparagus tips until tender. Drain and keep warm. In saucepan, combine 1 cup sauce and ½ cup milk. Set on medium heat. Stir in cheese and cook until melted. Add mustard or salt if desired.

When soufflé is done, invert on towel. Spoon ¼ cup sauce over one end. Put asparagus on and roll. Place seam side down onto platter. Pour remaining cheese sauce in separate dish and serve. Serves 6.

This is excellent served with fresh fruit, ham and rolls.

Asparagus Omelet

 2 eggs
 1 Tbsp. asparagus purée*
 ⅛ tsp. salt
   dash freshly ground pepper
 1½ Tbsp. corn oil
 1 Tbsp. grated parmesan cheese

Beat together eggs, asparagus purée, salt and pepper. Heat oil in omelet pan until very hot and oil starts to smoke. Pour egg mixture, swirling around until mixture coats the pan bottom. Keeping pan in motion, move it back and forth quickly, lift egg mixture with knife edge or spoon so uncooked portion flows underneath to cook. Cooking process should take 1 minute or less. Place cheese on half of omelet, fold in half and serve. Serves 1.

*Refer to Potpourri section

Asparagus Crepes

 24 asparagus spears, cleaned, trimmed and cooked
  8 crepes
    salt and pepper to taste
  1 Tbsp. butter
  1 cup Hollandaise sauce

Place 3 asparagus spears in the crepe, salt and pepper lightly; roll crepe. Place seam side down in buttered pyrex dish. Place in preheated 350° oven until warm. Pour Hollandaise sauce over and return to oven until bubbly. Serves 4.

Asparagus Quiche

    pastry for one-crust 9-inch pie
¾ lb. fresh asparagus or one 8 oz. pkg. frozen cut
    asparagus
3 eggs, beaten
1½ cups light cream or milk
¾ tsp. salt
    dash nutmeg
1½ cups shredded swiss cheese

Line 9-inch pie plate with pastry (do not prick pastry). Line shell with foil and fill it with dry beans. Bake in 450⁰ oven for 5 minutes. Remove from oven; remove foil and beans. Reduce oven temperature to 325⁰.

Cut asparagus into 1½-inch pieces. Cook asparagus pieces, uncovered until tender.

In medium bowl, combine eggs, cream or milk, salt and nutmeg. Stir in cooked asparagus. Sprinkle cheese in prebaked pastry shell. Pour egg mixture over. Bake for 35-40 minutes or until knife inserted comes out clean. Let stand 10 minutes before serving. Serves 6.

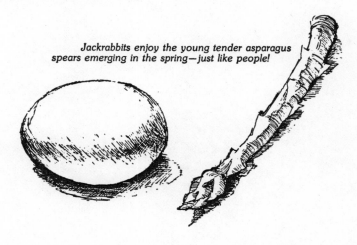

Jackrabbits enjoy the young tender asparagus spears emerging in the spring—just like people!

Chicken, Ham & Asparagus Quiche

    1 uncooked pie shell
    ¾ cup diced chicken or turkey
    ¼ cup diced ham
    2 cups (¾ lb.) asparagus, cut in ½-inch pieces and
      cooked
    1 cup grated swiss cheese
    3 eggs
 ½-¾ cup milk or cream
      pinch of EACH, nutmeg and pepper
  3-4 asparagus spears, cooked

Place into uncooked pie shell: chicken, ham, asparagus and grated swiss cheese. Break eggs into large measuring cup and add enough milk or cream to make 1¼ cups. Add a pinch of nutmeg and pepper and beat well with fork. Pour over mixture in pie shell, decorate with cooked asparagus spears. Bake at 425° for 15 minutes. Reduce heat to 300° and bake 30-40 minutes or until cold knife inserted into center comes out clean. Serves 4-6.

Asparagus Quick Crust Pie

egg bread or whole wheat bread slices
½ cup cooked and crumbled bacon
boiled ham
2 cups heavy cream
3 eggs
½ cup grated parmesan, swiss or jarlsberg cheese
1 cup (½ lb.) chopped, cooked asparagus

Line the bottom of a 10 or 12-inch pie dish with bread slices. Sprinkle the bacon over them. Combine cream, eggs, cheese and asparagus and mix until blended. Pour over the bread and bake in 350° oven for 30-40 minutes or until custard is puffed and firm. Serve hot or at room temperature. Serves 6-8.

Asparagus and Bacon Stir-Fry

5 slices bacon
2 Tbsp. bacon drippings
2 lbs. fresh asparagus, cut in ⅓-inch diagonal slices
1 Tbsp. minced onion
2 tsp. minced ginger root
1 8 oz. can water chestnuts, drained and sliced
¼ tsp. sesame oil

Fry bacon in skillet until crisp and golden. Remove bacon, cool and crumble. Drain all but 2 tablespoons drippings from skillet. Break woody ends from asparagus spears and cut spears into thin (⅓-inch) diagonal slices, leaving tips whole.

Heat bacon drippings in skillet over medium heat and sauté onion and ginger. Add asparagus and stir-fry until tender-crisp, about 5 minutes. Add bacon and water chestnuts. Stir-fry 2-3 minutes longer. Stir in sesame oil and serve. Serves 4-6.

Asparagus, Bacon and Egg Crepes

        2 Tbsp. butter
        2 Tbsp. flour
        1 cup milk
        1 Tbsp. minced onion
      ½ tsp. salt
      ½ tsp. dry mustard
    4-6 slices bacon, crisp cooked, crumbled
        6 hard-cooked eggs, chopped (reserve 1 yolk for
          garnish)
        8 crepes
        1 lb. asparagus, cooked

Melt butter, add flour, cook and stir over medium heat until bubbly. Add milk, onion, salt, dry mustard and cook until smooth and thickened. Stir in bacon and eggs and keep hot. Divide asparagus spears among crepes, letting tips stick out. Spoon sauce over asparagus on crepes and roll up. Sieve reserved egg yolk and use to garnish. Serves 4.

Ham-Asparagus Crepes with Mushroom Sauce

8 crepes (any size)
3 Tbsp. butter
2 jars (2½ oz. EACH) sliced mushrooms, drained
3 Tbsp. flour
1 cup water
2 tsp. instant chicken bouillon
⅓ cup cream or half and half
¼ cup shredded cheddar cheese
1 Tbsp. chopped chives
8 slices cooked ham, thinly sliced
4 big slices swiss cheese, halved
1 lb. asparagus spears, cleaned and cooked

Melt butter, add mushrooms and cook. Stir in flour, cook over medium heat until bubbly. Add water and bouillon, cook until thick. Blend in cream, cheese and chives. Keep hot. Put ham slice, cheese slice and 2-3 asparagus spears on each crepe and roll up. Arrange in greased 13x9 pan. Spoon sauce over crepes. Bake at 350° for 25 minutes. Serves 4.

Hawaiian Ham Roll-Ups

12 spears asparagus, fresh or frozen
6 slices boiled or baked ham
¼ cup butter
2 Tbsp. minced onion
2 cups half and half cream
⅓ cup flour
1 tsp. salt
½ cup grated sharp cheddar cheese

Cook fresh or frozen asparagus; drain. Roll two spears of asparagus in each slice of ham. Make a sauce of butter, onion, milk, flour, salt and cheese and pour over ham rolls. Bake at 350° for 20-25 minutes or until bubbly. Serves 6.

Asparagus Royale in Puff Shell

¼ lb. mushrooms, washed and sliced
¼ cup butter or margarine
¼ cup flour
¾ tsp. salt
    pinch sugar
1 cup milk (part asparagus liquid may be used)
1 egg, slightly beaten
¾ lb. asparagus, cut into 1-inch lengths, cooked
4 cream puff shells

Sauté mushrooms for 5 minutes in butter. Blend in the flour and seasonings and add milk gradually. Stir until mixture is smooth and thickened; pour some of the mixture over the beaten egg, mix and pour back. Add the asparagus and heat thoroughly, stirring carefully. Slice the top from each puff shell; fill with the hot mixture. Replace the top and serve immediately. Serves 4.

Asparagus and Ham Luncheon Dish

1 lb. fresh asparagus
2 Tbsp. butter
2 Tbsp. flour
1 cup milk
¼ tsp. salt
   pinch of sugar
½ tsp. prepared mustard
1 cup grated american cheese
½ lb. boiled or baked ham, lightly pan-fried

Wash, prepare and cook asparagus until tender. Meanwhile, make a white sauce by combining the melted butter and flour in the top of a double boiler and adding the milk gradually. Cook over hot water and stir until mixture is smooth and thickened. Blend in the salt, sugar and mustard, then add the cheese. Cook until cheese is melted. Arrange freshly cooked asparagus and ham attractively on a platter, then pour the sauce interestingly down through the center of the arrangement. Serve immediately. Serves 4.

Asparagus has been grown in American gardens since the earliest settlements were established. In Middlebury, Vermont, the Register of June 29, 1917, says, "There is an asparagus bed on the Elias Lyman farm at the 'Point', town of Hartford, which was started 101 years ago, and continues to this day to yield an annual and generous crop." It was not, however, until after 1850 or 1860 that asparagus was planted extensively by commercial growers in this country.

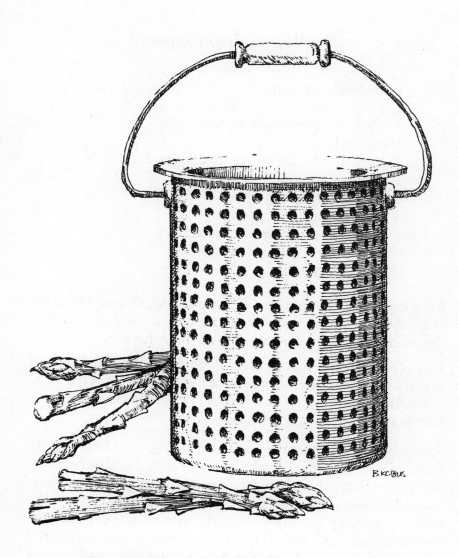

B KOBUS

SIDE DISHES

Scalloped Asparagus

1 lb. fresh asparagus
1 Tbsp. butter
1 Tbsp. all-purpose flour
1 cup milk
4 eggs, hard-cooked, finely chopped
1 Tbsp. butter
½ tsp. salt
¼ tsp. cayenne pepper
2 Tbsp. fine dry bread crumbs
½ cup (2 oz.) grated swiss cheese
2 Tbsp. butter

Bring large saucepan of salted water to boiling. Grease 1½ quart shallow baking dish. Boil cleaned asparagus until fork-tender. Drain; transfer to paper toweling to drain further.

To prepare cream sauce, melt 1 tablespoon butter in small saucepan. Stir in flour; cook 1 minute. Gradually stir in the milk. Cook, stirring constantly, until sauce thickens, about 3 minutes. Remove from heat; reserve sauce.

Arrange half of asparagus in a layer in prepared baking dish; sprinkle with half the chopped egg; dot with 1 tablespoon butter; season with salt and cayenne pepper. Arrange another layer with remaining asparagus. Sprinkle center portion with remaining chopped egg. Pour cream sauce down middle of casserole. Sprinkle sauce with bread crumbs and cheese. Dot uncovered portions of asparagus with remaining 2 tablespoons butter to prevent drying out during baking.

Bake covered in preheated 400° oven for 15 minutes. Uncover; bake 2-3 minutes or until top is browned. Serves 4.

Foiled Asparagus

1 lb. asparagus, cleaned and trimmed
salt and freshly ground pepper
1 Tbsp. butter
1/4-1/2 cup rich chicken stock

Place asparagus on large sheet of aluminum foil with edges folded to form a slight rim. Sprinkle asparagus with salt and pepper; dot with butter and carefuly pour stock over. Fold sides of foil over asparagus to form sealed cooking container. Bake at 400° for 20-30 minutes or until crisp-tender. Place on warmed serving dish and serve immediately. Serves 4.

Asparagus Casserole

2½ lbs. asparagus, cut into 2-inch pieces
3 cups white sauce
4 hard-boiled eggs
1 cup Grapenuts (not flakes)

Cook asparagus until tender. Drain and place in casserole dish. Season with salt and pepper. Cover with white sauce. Slice eggs and layer on top. Sprinkle Grapenuts over all. Bake at 300° until heated through, about ½ hour. Serves 12.

Asparagus Toast Rolls

16 bread slices
1 lb. asparagus, cooked
   cheese sauce*

Trim crusts from large slices of fresh white bread, curve opposite edges of the slice upward so as to come together, and fasten with toothpicks. Toast on all sides in broiler or hot oven, watching carefully. Fill toast rolls with drained hot asparagus and arrange on platter. Serve with cheese sauce. Two asparagus rolls will serve 1. Serves 8.

*Refer to Sauces and Dressing

Asparagus in White Wine

32 asparagus spears, cooked
 8 oz. ham, cooked and sliced in 1 oz. slices
 2 Tbsp. butter or margarine, melted
½ cup white wine
 1 tsp. dried dill weed
   grated parmesan cheese, as desired

Halve each ham slice. Wrap 2 asparagus spears in halved ham slice. Fasten with toothpick, place in pan. Combine butter, wine and dill. Spoon over asparagus. Sprinkle with cheese. Bake at 370° for 8 minutes, basting with sauce. Makes 16 rolls.

Sesame Asparagus

2 lbs. fresh asparagus or 20 oz. frozen spears
1 Tbsp. sesame seeds
2 Tbsp. pure vegetable oil
1 cup thinly sliced onion (1 large)
1 tsp. salt
¼ tsp. pepper
1 Tbsp. soy sauce

Slice cleaned asparagus into ¼-inch thick diagonal slices (for frozen spears, cut into 2-inch pieces).

Heat sesame seeds in skillet over medium-high heat until golden brown, shaking pan frequently. Remove to bowl. Add oil to pan. Heat over high heat. Add onion. Fry 1 minute, stirring constantly. Add asparagus. Fry 3 minutes or until just tender, stirring frequently. Stir in salt, pepper, soy sauce and sesame seeds. Serves 8.

Almond Asparagus

1½ lbs. fresh asparagus
⅓ cup almonds
1 Tbsp. salad oil
½ tsp. salt
⅛ tsp. pepper
⅛ tsp. sugar
several shakes ground ginger

Slice cleaned asparagus in 1½-inch diagonal pieces. Sauté almonds in oil until light golden in medium skillet; add asparagus, salt, pepper, sugar and ginger. Cover, turn heat to high and cook over medium-high heat, shaking pan to prevent sticking or burning. Cook just until asparagus is fork tender, about 5 minutes. Serve promptly. Serves 6.

"Stuffy" Asparagus

1 cup herb seasoned stuffing mix
¼ cup butter or margarine, melted
1 2 oz. jar sliced mushrooms, drained (save liquid)
2 cups (½ lb.) fresh asparagus, cooked
2 Tbsp. sliced green onions
¼ cup butter
2 Tbsp. flour
½ tsp. salt
½ tsp. dry mustard
   dash of white pepper
1 cup half and half
¼ cup grated parmesan cheese

Combine stuffing mix with ¼ cup butter and drained mushroom liquid. Line bottom of 9-inch pie pan with stuffing mix. Top with asparagus. Sauté onion and mushrooms in remaining ¼ cup butter. Stir in flour, salt, dry mustard and pepper. Gradually stir in half and half. Cook over low heat, stirring constantly. Pour sauce over asparagus, sprinkle with cheese. Bake at 375° for 15 minutes. Serves 4-6.

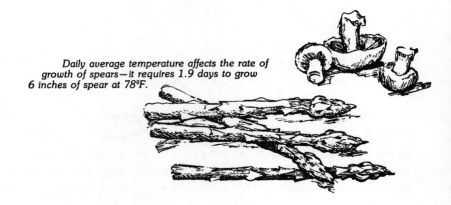

Daily average temperature affects the rate of growth of spears—it requires 1.9 days to grow 6 inches of spear at 78°F.

Asparagus-Potato Tart (Low Calorie)

1½ lb. potatoes
    salt
    basil leaves
1 medium onion, sliced thin
1 10 oz. package frozen or 1 lb. fresh asparagus, cooked
3 medium tomatoes, sliced
1 Tbsp. parmesan cheese

Peel potatoes and slice ⅛-inch thick. Place half of potato slices in greased 9-inch square baking dish. Sprinkle with salt and basil. Add layers of sliced onion, asparagus and tomato slices, sprinkling each layer with salt and basil. Top with remaining potato slices; sprinkle with parmesan cheese. Cover with foil. Bake at 375° for 40 minutes. Remove cover and continue baking 10-15 minutes longer or until potatoes are tender. Serves 6.

Brown Sugar Asparagus

4 Tbsp. butter
1 Tbsp. brown sugar
2 cups cut-up asparagus
1-1½ cups rich chicken stock

Melt butter in skillet, add sugar and stir until sugar is dissolved. Add asparagus and sauté 2 minutes (be careful it does not burn). Add the chicken stock, cover and cook over medium-low heat 3 minutes. Cook uncovered for 2 minutes to reduce sauce. Serve hot. Serves 4.

Layered Asparagus Casserole

2 cups (1½ lbs.) diced fresh asparagus
1 can cream of mushroom soup
¼ cup almond slices
  onion rings

Make 2 layers in casserole dish in the following order: asparagus on bottom, next mushroom soup, almonds and onion rings. Repeat layers. Bake at 350° for 45 minutes. Serves 4.

Asparagus Supreme

1½ lbs. fresh asparagus
1 can cream of chicken soup
1 Tbsp. flour
½ cup sour cream
¼ cup grated carrot
1 Tbsp. grated onion
  salt and pepper
¾ cup herb seasoned stuffing mix
2 Tbsp. butter, melted

Clean and trim the asparagus, cut into 1-inch pieces and cook in boiling water until tender. Drain. Blend together soup and flour. Add sour cream, carrot, onion, salt and pepper. Stir in asparagus. Turn into a 2-quart casserole. Combine stuffing mix and melted butter; sprinkle around edge of baking dish. Bake at 350° for 30 minutes. Serves 8.

Asparagus with Water Chestnuts (Microwave)

⅓ cup margarine or butter
¾ tsp. salt
⅛ tsp. pepper
7 cups (2-3 lbs.) asparagus, cut in 1-inch diagonal pieces
1 can (8 oz.) water chestnuts, drained and sliced

Place margarine, salt, pepper and asparagus in 2-quart casserole. Cover tightly and microwave on high (100%) 7 minutes.

Stir in water chestnuts. Microwave uncovered on high (100%) until asparagus is crisp-tender, 5-7 minutes longer. Serves 10.

Hungarian Style Asparagus

2 lbs. asparagus
  salted water
1 tsp. sugar
3 Tbsp. butter
1 pint sour cream
½ cup bread crumbs

Add sugar to salted water and boil asparagus until tender. Drain. Butter ovenproof dish. Layer half the sour cream and bread crumbs. Top with asparagus. Finish layers with sour cream and bread crumbs. Bake at 350° for 30 minutes. Serves 8.

Poached Vegetable Bundles

    6 cups water
    2 Tbsp. chicken bouillon granules
    1 tsp. minced dried onion
    6 large romaine or spinach leaves
    2 medium carrots, cut into 4-inch sticks
    1 lb. asparagus spears
   18 whole green beans
      creamy Hollandaise sauce
(In place of some of the vegetables, green onions, celery sticks
or broccoli spears can be used)

*In skillet combine water, bouillon granules and dried onion; bring
to boiling, stirring to dissolve bouillon. Cut heavy center vein
out of romaine or spinach leaves. Immerse leaves in hot broth
for a few seconds, just until limp; drain. Fold each leaf in thirds
lengthwise. Divide carrot sticks, asparagus and green beans into
six bundles. Wrap a romaine leaf around the center of each;
secure with a wooden pick if necessary.*

*Place vegetable bundles in broth. Bring broth to boiling; reduce
heat; cover and simmer about 12 minutes or until vegetables
are tender-crisp. Lift bundles from broth with slotted spatula
to serving platter. Spoon creamy Hollandaise sauce over
bundles. Serves 6.*

Early writers praised the taste of the wild over the cultivated form of asparagus. Pomponius, who lived in the second century noted the existence of both forms and said, "The wild asparagus is more pleasant to eat." Palladius, an author of the third century, praises the sweetness of the wild form found growing among rocks. Along with this preference there was a rationale, "Nature has made the asparagus wild so that anyone may gather as found," wrote Pliny in the first century.

Boswell acknowledges the preference of the ancients for the wild over the cultivated form or the cultivated form grown from wild seeds or plants, but he says, "Such progress in development had been made (by 200 A.D.) that the cultivated forms were consistently as good as the best wild plants."

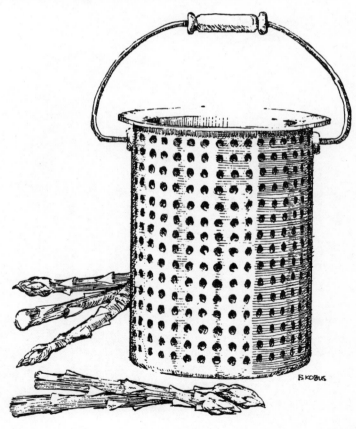

SAUCES
and
DRESSINGS

Sour Cream Dressing

1 cup sour cream
2 Tbsp. minced onion
2 tsp. sugar
1 Tbsp. vinegar
½ tsp. capers
½ tsp. paprika
1 tsp. salt

Mix all ingredients together and chill. Serve over chilled asparagus spears. 1 cup croutons can be folded into dressing before serving, or sprinkled over the top.

Boiled Salad Dressing

2 Tbsp. flour
1 Tbsp. sugar
½ tsp. EACH salt, paprika and dry mustard
2 egg yolks, slightly beaten
½ cup milk
¼ cup vinegar
2 Tbsp. butter
parsley, chives or capers

Combine flour, sugar and seasonings in saucepan. Combine milk and egg yolk; stir in flour mixture. Cook over medium heat, stirring until mixture boils and thickens. Boil 1 minute. Remove from heat; stir in vinegar and butter. Sprinkle with minced parsley, chives or capers. Chill. It may be thinned with sour cream. Makes about 1½ cups.

Yogurt-Herb Dressing

1 8 oz. carton plain yogurt
2 tsp. chopped parsley
1 tsp. prepared mustard
1 tsp. chopped chives
½ tsp. dried tarragon leaves
½ tsp. salt
¼ tsp. paprika
   dash cayenne pepper

Mix all ingredients and refrigerate at least 1 hour. Just before serving, toss chilled asparagus with dressing and arrange in lettuce-lined bowl. Garnish with parsley and cherry tomatoes, if desired.

Sauces are for serving over hot asparagus. Dressings are for serving over cold asparagus.

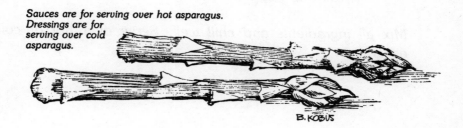

B. KOBUS

Chilled Green Dressing

⅓ cup olive oil
1 cup chopped parsley
1 egg, hard-cooked
2 tsp. EACH capers and minced onion
3 Tbsp. lemon juice
1 garlic clove, chopped
1 anchovy filet
½ tsp. salt
½ tsp. basil leaves
   pepper to taste

Put all ingredients in blender and blend until smooth. Chill well.
Serve over asparagus.

Yogurt Onion Dressing

½ small onion, minced
1 cup unflavored yogurt
2 tsp. minced fresh mint leaves
¼ tsp. cumin powder
   salt and pepper to taste

Mix all ingredients and chill well. Serve over hot or cold
asparagus.

1-Step Cheese Sauce

½ cup mayonnaise
½ cup milk
½ cup shredded cheddar or american or grated
parmesan, or crumbled blue cheese

*Stir together mayonnaise, milk and cheese in small saucepan.
Heat over medium-low heat about 5 minutes or until heated.
Serve over hot asparagus.*

Continental Lemon Sauce

1 cup mayonnaise
2 eggs
3 Tbsp. lemon juice
½ tsp. salt
½ tsp. dry mustard

*In small saucepan with wire whisk, stir together mayonnaise,
eggs, lemon juice, salt and dry mustard until smooth. Stir over
medium-low heat until thick (do not boil). Sprinkle with paprika.
Serve over hot asparagus.*

Sour Cream Sauce

1 cup sour cream
1 tsp. prepared mustard
2 tsp. lemon juice
¼ tsp. salt

*Combine all ingredients and heat over very low heat, stirring
occasionally, until warm. For variation, 1 cup mayonnaise may
be added if desired. Serve over hot asparagus.*

Hollandaise Sauce

  1/2 cup butter or margarine
      juice of 1/2 lemon
  1/8 salt
    3 egg yolks

Melt butter or margarine until bubbly. Add lemon juice and salt. Add slowly to egg yolks, beating constantly. Serve over hot asparagus.

Anchovy Butter

  1/2 can (2 oz) anchovy fillets
  1/3 cup butter or margarine
    3 Tbsp. lemon juice
  1/2 clove garlic, crushed
      dash cayenne pepper
    2 Tbsp. snipped parsley

Rinse anchovies and drain on paper toweling; mash. Melt butter in small saucepan. Stir in anchovies, lemon juice, garlic and pepper. Cook over medium heat, stirring constantly, until hot. Stir in parsley. Serve over hot asparagus.

Herb Butter

½ cup butter or margarine, melted
2 Tbsp. finely chopped parsley
1 Tbsp. snipped chives
½ tsp. dried tarragon leaves
2 Tbsp. lemon juice

In small bowl, combine melted butter, parsley, chives, tarragon and lemon juice. Stir until well blended. Serve over hot asparagus.

Caraway-Sour Cream Sauce

2 Tbsp. butter or margarine
1 Tbsp. flour
1 cup sour cream
1½ tsp. fresh lemon juice
¾ tsp. salt
$\frac{1}{16}$ tsp. ground black pepper
2 tsp. caraway seeds
    fresh parsley

Melt butter in saucepan. Blend in flour. Stir in sour cream and cook only until medium thickness, 3-4 minutes. Add lemon juice, salt, pepper and caraway seed. Mix well. Serve over hot asparagus. Garnish with parsley.

Lemon Sauce

2 Tbsp. butter or margarine
2 Tbsp. flour
¼ cup fresh or frozen lemon juice
1 cup boiling water (from asparagus)
¼ tsp. salt
    dash of Tabasco
½ cup dairy sour cream
1 Tbsp. butter, melted

Melt butter or margarine in saucepan. Stir in flour and cook 2 minutes. Add lemon juice and water. Stir and cook until smooth and thickened. Simmer 5 minutes; add salt and Tabasco. Just before serving, add sour cream and melted butter. Serve over hot asparagus.

Lemon-Sesame Seed Sauce

¼ cup butter or margarine
½ lemon (juice and grated peeling)
1 Tbsp. toasted sesame seed
1 tsp. sugar
¼ tsp. garlic salt

Melt butter or margarine. Add grated peel and juice of ½ lemon, sesame seed, sugar and garlic salt; heat. Serve over hot asparagus.

Easy Chive Sauce

1 3 oz. package chive cream cheese
1 Tbsp. milk

In small saucepan, combine cream cheese and milk. Stir over very low heat until warm and smooth. Serve over hot asparagus.

Polonaise

½ cup butter or margarine
⅓ cup fine dry bread crumbs
2 hard-cooked eggs, finely chopped
1 Tbsp. chopped parsley
½ tsp. dried savory leaves
½ tsp. salt
⅛ tsp. pepper

Heat butter in heavy saucepan over low heat, stirring until amber colored. Stir in bread crumbs; remove from heat. Stir in half the eggs. Add parsley, savory, salt and pepper. Place mixture over hot asparagus. Garnish with remaining egg.

In Roman times, asparagus was not only eaten "in season" but was dried for later use. It was simply and quickly prepared by boiling the dried shoots.

Sweet Asparagus Vinaigrette

  2 lbs. asparagus
  1 tsp. salt
$\frac{1}{8}$ tsp. pepper
   dash of cayenne
$\frac{1}{4}$ tsp. paprika
  3 Tbsp. tarragon vinegar
$\frac{1}{2}$ cup salad oil
  1 Tbsp. minced green pepper
  1 Tbsp. chopped sweet pickle
  1 Tbsp. minced parsley
  2 tsp. chopped green onion or chives

Wash and trim asparagus. Steam until tender. Drain and chill. Mix remaining ingredients and chill. When ready to serve, arrange asparagus on a serving plate or on lettuce leaves that have been arranged on a plate and pour oil and vinegar mixture over asparagus. Serves 6.

Sour Cream-Horseradish Sauce

  1 Tbsp. prepared horseradish
  1 cup sour cream
   salt and pepper

Combine all ingredients and heat over very low heat until warm. Serve over cooked asparagus and sprinkle with browned bread crumbs.

Egg Sauce

3 Tbsp. butter
3 Tbsp. flour
1 tsp. salt
2 cups milk
¼ tsp. onion juice
few drops Worcestershire sauce
1 tsp. lemon juice, if desired
4 hard-cooked eggs, coarsely chopped

Melt butter, blend in flour and salt, and add milk; stir over direct heat until sauce boils and thickens. Add Worcestershire sauce, lemon juice and onion juice. Just before serving, fold in chopped eggs. Serves 5.

Roasted Pepper Cream

½ cup chopped red peppers, roasted and patted dry
2 Tbsp. butter or margarine
¾ cup heavy cream

In medium skillet sauté pepper in butter over low heat, stirring occasionally, 5 minutes. Stir in cream until well blended; heat through. Serve over hot asparagus.

Wine Sauce

1 cup white sauce
3 Tbsp. dry white wine
1-2 tsp. parmesan cheese

Stir dry white wine into white sauce. Add parmesan cheese. Heat well and spoon over hot asparagus. Sprinkle with toasted slivered almonds.

Browned Butter Sauce

1 stick butter (¼ lb.)
2 Tbsp. lemon juice

In heavy pan, brown butter until golden, being careful that it does not brown too much. Remove from heat and cool for a few minutes. Stir in lemon juice. Serve over hot asparagus which has been sprinkled with grated parmesan or swiss cheese.

Sauce Delicious

¼ cup French dressing
1 hard-cooked egg, minced
1 pimento, minced
1 Tbsp. minced parsley

Heat dressing over low heat and add remaining ingredients. Serve over hot asparagus.

White and green asparagus come from the same plant. The difference is achieved by different harvest methods. White asparagus is harvested prior to the emergence of the spears from the bed that has been mounded. The cutter will probe below the soil surface to find the spear. Once the spear emerges from the bed, the spear will turn green when exposed to light. The green spear is only cut several inches below the soil surface, hence the white "butt" portion on the bottom of the green stalk.

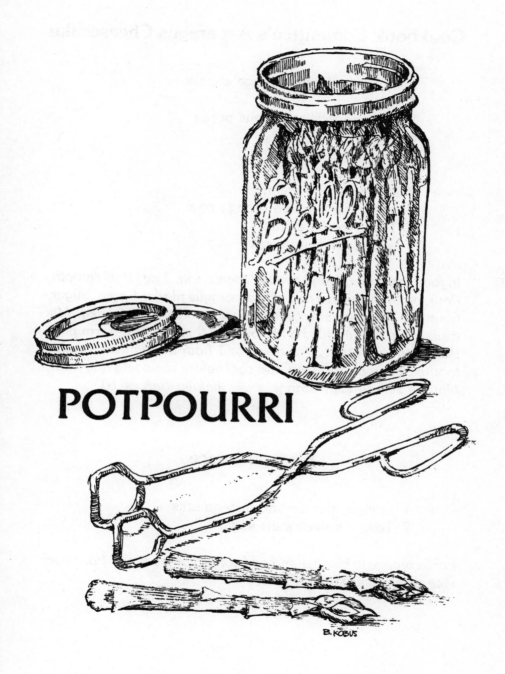

POTPOURRI

B. KOBUS

Cookbook Committee's Asparagus Cheesecake

2 pints small curd cottage cheese
1 egg
2 cups smooth asparagus purée
6 eggs
1⅓ cups sugar
½ cup flour
¼ cup whipping cream
2 Tbsp. fresh grated orange peel
2 Tbsp. vanilla extract
¼ tsp. ground nutmeg

In food processor, blend cottage cheese with 1 egg until smooth. Pour into mixing bowl and add asparagus purée, 6 eggs, sugar, flour, whipping cream, orange peel, vanilla and nutmeg. Mix well. Pour into an oiled and floured 10-inch spring-form pan. Bake in a preheated 375° oven for 1 hour 20 minutes, or until toothpick comes out clean. Let cool before removing ring form. May be served with orange sauce below. Serves 10.

Orange Sauce

1 orange, peeled and in segments
2 Tbsp. confectioners sugar

Purée orange in blender and add confectioners sugar. Pour over slice of cheesecake and serve.

Asparagus Drop Cookies

1 cup grated asparagus
1 tsp. soda
1 cup sugar
1 cup butter or margarine
1 egg, beaten
2 cups flour
1 tsp. cinnamon
½ tsp. EACH cloves, nutmeg and salt
1 cup chopped nuts
1 cup raisins (optional)

Beat together thoroughly the asparagus, soda, sugar and shortening. Add egg. Beat well. Sift flour and spices. Add dry ingredients, mix well. Add nuts and raisins. Drop by teaspoonful on greased baking sheet. Bake at 375° for 12-15 minutes. Makes 3 dozen cookies.

Asparagus Ice Cream

10 large eggs
2 cups sugar
4 cups whipping cream
2 cups milk
2 cups asparagus purée
dash salt
vanilla to taste

In blender, blend together eggs and sugar. Blend until sugar dissolves. Pour into large bowl. Combine egg mixture with cream, milk, purée, salt and vanilla. Pour into ice cream freezer. Process until finished. Makes 1 gallon.

Asparagus-Lime Pie

Crust:
9-inch pie crust, baked 20 minutes at 350°, filled with foil and dry beans to prevent shrinkage; then cooled

Filling:
- 3 eggs, separated
- ½ cup sugar
- ¼ cup fresh lime juice
- 2 tsp. grated lime peel
- ½ tsp. salt
- 2 cups smooth asparagus purée*
- ½ cup sugar

Combine egg yolks, ½ cup sugar, lime juice, lime peel and salt in the top of a double boiler and beat until well blended. Place over simmering water. Stir constantly; cook until thickened and coats a spoon. Remove from the heat and fold in asparagus purée. Beat egg whites until stiff, adding ½ cup sugar while beating. Fold egg whites into filling. Fill cooled crust with filling and bake in preheated 325° oven for 30 minutes. Let cool on a rack. Serves 8.

Asparagus purée can be made by boiling asparagus, draining well, then processing in blender to purée.

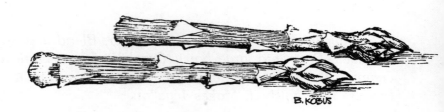

B. KOBUS

Asparagus Bread

   3 eggs
   1 cup oil
1⅔ cups sugar
   1 cup brown sugar
   2 tsp. vanilla
   2 cups (¾ lb.) asparagus, cleaned and grated

In separate bowl mix:
   3 cups flour
 ¼ tsp. baking powder
   1 tsp. salt
   1 tsp. soda
   3 tsp. cinnamon
 ½ cup chopped nuts
   1 cup raisins (optional)

Beat eggs until light and foamy. Add oil, sugar, brown sugar, vanilla and asparagus; mix lightly. Add flour mixture and blend. Add nuts and raisins. Bake in greased loaf pan 325° for 1 hour or until done. Makes 2–5 x 9 loaves.

Asparagus Tea

Do not throw that asparagus cooking water away! After asparagus is cooked to your taste, get out your favorite mug. When draining asparagus, pour your "asparagus tea" in your mug. If unsalted, add salt and pepper to taste. A pat of butter on top or a sprinkle of cheese adds a good flavor. Don't be surprised if "asparagus tea" becomes a regular routine every time you prepare asparagus!

Asparagus Pasta

    3 cups unbleached flour
    1 tsp. salt
    4 eggs, beaten
    ½ cup asparagus purée

Sift the flour and salt onto a wooden board and make a well in the center. Combine the eggs and asparagus in a blender and blend until smooth (or beat with a whisk until smooth). Put the asparagus mixture into the well formed by the flour and work in the flour with your fingers until a smooth dough is formed. Then knead the dough until very smooth and elastic, about 10 minutes, adding 2-4 tablespoons flour as you knead. Cover dough with plastic wrap or a bowl and let rest for at least 10 minutes (20 minutes is better).

To make the noodles by hand, divide the dough into 2 pieces and on a lightly floured board, flatten each of the pieces into an oblong shape with the palm of your hand. Then roll out each piece as thinly as possible by rolling and turning the dough as you work. Sprinkle lightly with flour and let the dough rest for 10 minutes; then roll each portion into a jelly-roll shape and cut the dough into crosswise strips, ½-inch wide.

Once the noodles have been cut, spread them on a clean cloth and let dry for about 1 hour. Then cook them in a large kettle of salted boiling water (1 tablespoon salt per gallon of water) for about 5-7 minutes, or until al dente. Makes 1 pound fresh noodles.

Dried Noodles

Lay the noodles on a clean cloth and turn them every few hours until they are completely dry. You may also hang noodles that are over 18 inches in length over the back of a chair or on the handles of wooden spoons that have been secured by closing the bowl of the spoon in a drawer. Do not attempt to dry the noodles in too hot a room or they will crack. Dried noodles will keep for weeks in airtight containers of metal, glass or plastic. This recipe will make 12 ounces dried noodles.

Asparagus Cordial

4 cups (1¼ lb.) asparagus, cleaned and cut up
4 cups sugar dissolved in 2 cups water
½ cup lime juice
1 one-fifth bottle of Vodka

Let stand at least 30 days. Add green food coloring for color. Place in one gallon glass container.

Asparagus Sweet Pickles

2-4 lbs. asparagus
2 cups vinegar
1 cup water
½ cup sugar
1 tsp. whole allspice
6 whole cloves
3 inches stick cinnamon

Wash asparagus. Trim to fit pint jars. Cover asparagus with boiling water; cook 3 minutes; drain. Pack length-wise into hot pint jars, leaving ½-inch headspace. In a saucepan combine vinegar, water and sugar. Tie allspice, cloves and cinnamon in a cheesecloth bag. Add spice bag to pickling liquid. Simmer 15 minutes. Cover asparagus with hot pickling liquid leaving ½-inch head space. Adjust lids. Process in boiling water bath 10 minutes. Makes 4 pints.

Pickled Asparagus

Brine:
3 quarts water
2 quarts white vinegar
10 Tbsp. canning salt (non-iodized)
2 Tbsp. pickling spice (without cloves)

Boil the water, vinegar, salt and pickling spices. Blanch asparagus for 1 minute in boiling water and cool in ice water immediately. Pack tightly in prepared 1-quart canning jars (20-25 spears). Leave ½-inch headspace. Insert 1 clove of garlic in jar and fill with hot brine, covering the tips. Seal with hot lids which have been boiled and kept hot. Seal tightly. Store until ready to use. Brine will fill 4-5 quarts.

Makes great Christmas gifts

Plumosus or asparagus fern is widely used by florists for sprays in floral arrangements.

Several climbing species of asparagus are grown as house plants and in greenhouses for their ornamental foliage. The fern, **A. plumosus,** is especially elegant and is highly prized for its delicate feathery branches. The most noticeable characteristic of all asparagus is the absence of true leaves.

Index

ORDER FORM

To order make your check or money order payable to Stockton Asparagus Festival and mail to:

Stockton Asparagus Festival
46 W. Fremont Street
Stockton CA 95202

Please send me:

_____ copy(ies) of Asparagus *All Ways . . . Always* Cookbook. $7.75 paperback edition ISBN 0-89087-487-5.

_____ copy(ies) of Asparagus *All Ways . . . Always* Cookbook. $9.95 spiral bound edition ISBN 0-89087-537-5.

$ _____ Total for Books

$ _____ Shipping Charges (@$1.00 shipping first book; 50¢ each additional book)

$ _____ California residents please add 6% sales tax

$ _____ Total Amount Enclosed

Name _____

Street Address: _____

City: _____ State: _____ Zip: _____

Other Asparagus Festival items are available such as posters, aprons, T-shirts, sweatshirts, caps, visors, tote bags, etc. For more information and prices on such items, write to the Stockton Asparagus Festival at the above address.

A WORD FROM THE PUBLISHER ...

Celestial Arts is the publisher of many excellent cookbooks, as well as books on topics of personal growth and health. Among our fine cookbooks are *The Garlic Lovers' Cookbook (Volumes I and II), The Artichoke Cookbook, The Avocado Lovers' Cookbook, The Vanilla Cookbook,* and *The Greengrocer Cookbook.* We also publish children's books and a complete line of posters/graphics. For a copy of our free catalog, please write to us or phone: Celestial Arts Publishing, P.O. Box 7327, Berkeley, CA 94707; (415) 524-1801.

TO HELP FIND YOUR WAY ...

The annual Stockton Asparagus Festival is held at the Oak Grove Regional Park. To learn the dates of this year's festival, please call (209) 943-1987 or within California (800) 821-4441. Or write to: Stockton Asparagus Festival, 46 West Fremont Street, Stockton, CA 95202.

And when you're ready to go, here's a map showing the location of Oak Grove Regional Park near Stockton.

Festival Access Routes

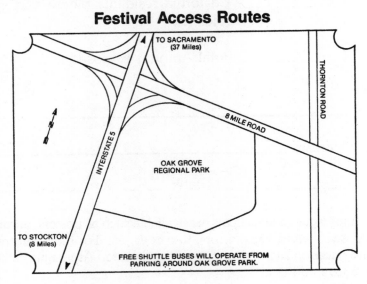